WHEN
THE
LIGHT
FINDS
US

WHEN THE LIGHT FINDS US

From a Life Sentence to a Life Transformed

JUDY HENDERSON

with *Jimmy Soni*

WORTHY
PUBLISHING

New York   Nashville

Worthy
Hachette Book Group
1290 Avenue of the Americas, New York, NY 10104
worthypublishing.com
@WorthyPub

First Edition: February 2025

Worthy is a division of Hachette Book Group, Inc. The Worthy name and logo are registered trademarks of Hachette Book Group, Inc.

The publisher is not responsible for websites (or their content) that are not owned by the publisher.

The Hachette Speakers Bureau provides a wide range of authors for speaking events. To find out more, go to hachettespeakersbureau.com or email HachetteSpeakers@hbgusa.com.

Worthy books may be purchased in bulk for business, educational, or promotional use. For information, please contact your local bookseller or the Hachette Book Group Special Markets Department at special.markets@hbgusa.com.

Scripture quotations are taken from the Holy Bible, New International Version®, NIV®. Copyright ©1973, 1978, 1984, 2011 by Biblica, Inc.™ Used by permission of Zondervan. All rights reserved worldwide. www.zondervan.com The "NIV" and "New International Version" are trademarks registered in the United States Patent and Trademark Office by Biblica, Inc.™

LCCN: 2024947173

ISBNs: 9781546006787 (hardcover), 9781546006800 (ebook)

Printed in the United States of America

LSC-C

Printing 1, 2025

For my family
—J.H.

For Jessica
—J.S.

Author's Note

The flaws and triumphs shared in these pages belong to real people, and their stories deserve careful handling. With this in mind, I've cross-checked facts against court documents, personal journals, interviews with family and friends, and various public and private records to ensure accuracy. Some names have been changed to protect privacy. My hope is that those whose stories are told here will recognize themselves and feel their journeys have been portrayed with grace. For, in the end, we are all broken and we are all worthy nonetheless.

Prologue

Imagine losing everything you love in a single day—your home, your children, your freedom. The pain drops you to your knees. But as your tears dry, you face a choice: Stay broken, or stand up and rebuild.

But I'm getting a little ahead of myself. My name is Judy Henderson. In 1982, at thirty-two, I was sent to prison for life. The crime? A murder I didn't commit.

It took thirty-six years for the truth to come out. I was sixty-eight when I was finally freed and pardoned. By then, I'd spent more time behind bars than I had in the free world.

This is my story.

Before my life took an unthinkable turn, I was living the quintessential American dream. My days revolved around my two children, Chip and Angel, in our modest suburban home. Our calendar was filled with dance recitals, barbecues, and birthday parties—the ordinary joys of family life.

Like many, I faced challenges. A difficult marriage ended

in divorce, but my children and I found happiness in our new normal. We were building a life filled with laughter and love.

Then Greg entered my world. Charming and charismatic, he swept me off my feet. Despite the red flags that now seem so obvious in hindsight, I fell for him, ignoring the instincts that whispered caution.

One day, Greg approached me with what seemed like a simple request. He needed to confront a man named Harry about an unresolved financial matter. Naively, I agreed to help, unaware that I was blind to his true plans.

What Greg had planned was far from a simple confrontation. In a horrifying turn of events, he robbed and murdered Harry in cold blood. The sound of the gunshot and the sight of Harry falling to the ground are seared into my memory.

In the chaos that followed, Greg manipulated the narrative, framing me for his crime. Despite my clean record and evidence supporting my innocence, the justice system failed me. In a cruel twist of fate, I was convicted of Harry's murder, while Greg walked free.

The courtroom scene plays in my mind like a recurring nightmare. As the judge sentenced me to life in prison without parole, my family's anguished cries filled the air. In that moment, the world I held dear all vanished in an instant.

Prison was a foreign land with its own brutal language. Danger lurked everywhere: shanks fashioned from toothbrushes glinted in shadows, invisible lines separated rival gangs, and violence could erupt at any moment.

At first, I tried to disappear. I'd mumble apologies for the slightest bump into another inmate, my eyes glued to the floor. But it was impossible to be invisible in these crowded confines. My middle-class background and soft-spoken manner might as well have been targets on my back. Worse, my attempts to hide screamed weakness—a death sentence in this unforgiving world. Despite every instinct, I had to adapt. I learned to meet stares with unflinching eyes, to stand my ground in the lunch line, to let my voice carry an edge of threat.

The prison system offered no sanctuary. It wasn't interested in rehabilitation, only punishment. We were systematically stripped of our names, our stories, our very humanity. We became mere numbers, faceless entities to be processed and controlled. Even the guards, sworn to protect, reveled in casual cruelties, shoving us along like cattle.

Hope felt like a luxury I couldn't afford. Survival became my sole focus. Some nights, lying on my thin mattress, listening to muffled sobs and angry whispers, the weight of this new reality nearly crushed me.

Yet, even in prison's bleakness, there were pinpricks of light. We found small ways to rebel—trading contraband, makeup, or hair color. These actions may have seemed insignificant to outsiders, but they gave us precious moments of control on the inside.

Humor kept us from despair, and silly jokes broke the monotony. We'd mimic the guards when their backs were turned and create absurd nicknames for the bland prison food.

We crafted celebrations using crude cakes made of hoarded snacks, and lukewarm tea served in chipped mugs became toasts of defiance. These weren't mere distractions; they were declarations. In these moments, we transcended our assigned prison numbers and criminal records. We were human, clinging to joy and connection against all odds.

"You do the time, or the time does you," prisoners say. I chose to do the time.

For three decades, I rebuilt myself through education, faith, therapy, and service. I earned my GED, then a paralegal certification. I devoured entire libraries, arming myself with knowledge against the ever-present threat of violence.

Faith anchored me. In the depths of confinement, I discovered spiritual freedom: a newfound purpose beyond iron bars and concrete walls.

Through thousands of hours of therapy, counseling, and meditation, I learned to turn raw emotion into action. I wrote anger-fueled letters to legislators, my words my weapons. In my sadness, I taught fellow inmates.

I became an advocate, fighting for prison reforms and protections for abused women. From behind bars, I testified before state legislators, giving voice to the voiceless.

Against the grinding routine of prison life, I found refuge in exercise. I led fitness classes, each push-up and squat a small victory.

This metamorphosis wasn't easy. Past traumas had

scarred me, and prison threatened to claim what remained. But I refused to yield.

Always, I remembered I wasn't just an inmate; I was a mom. Prison didn't erase my identity as a mother. It forced me to reimagine it.

I became a voice on the phone, a lifeline of love and guidance. When my daughter struggled to make pancakes, I walked her through each step, the prison phone pressed to my ear. As she navigated the maze of dating, I shared some of my own young missteps, hoping to spare her similar heartaches.

These fragments of motherhood kept me connected to my family and my true self. They strengthened my vow: I would speak to my children as a free woman once again, my name cleared.

To some, this seemed like pure fantasy. I had a life sentence without parole. Fellow lifers urged me to accept reality—to resign myself to dying behind bars. I refused. Call it blind faith or naive delusion, but I clung to my innocence and the belief that justice would prevail.

At every turn, I petitioned the state for my freedom. I crafted and recrafted clemency pleas. I spent thousands of hours with lawyers, mastering every intricacy of the legal system.

For thirty-five years, every one of those petitions failed. But in my thirty-sixth year of incarceration, my plea was granted. The governor himself arrived to deliver the news and apologize for the lifetime stolen from me.

As I stepped through that prison doorway into my family's arms, I saw that the world had become a foreign place after so many years of confinement. But I was free.

The woman who walked out of prison still resembled the one who had entered, with scars on her skin and wounds behind her eyes. Inside, though, she had been transformed.

Prison had weakened my relationships and stolen some of my identity. Yet through that struggle, I rebuilt myself into someone I never imagined I could become. I entered bitter; I left better. I arrived powerless; I departed powerful.

My story is rare. While I won my freedom, thousands of women remain behind bars—their pain unnoticed, their potential fading. I share my journey not just to highlight my triumph, but to illuminate their forgotten suffering.

Like mine, many of their lives are rooted in childhood trauma and abuse, destructive patterns repeating in adulthood. It's tempting to lie about our past; I did for years. But in honest storytelling, we claim a freedom beyond any court's decree: we have the power to define ourselves. We can shed labels imposed on us by others or by circumstances. We can choose to be victors, not victims.

This book is the story of that choice. If you feel trapped by circumstances beyond your control, may my journey offer you hope. Better yet, may it help you build that hope for yourself. Because hope isn't discovered by chance, like a dollar on a sidewalk. It is something we forge through unwavering devotion and iron discipline. During my incarceration, I discovered that hope is built from faith, too.

This hope sustained me, and it led me to a profound truth: When everything is stripped away, we face a final, crucial choice. We can surrender to darkness, or bravely shape our suffering into light. We are always, always free to choose.

I am Judy Henderson—thirty-six years a prisoner but forever free. And this is my story.

PART I

CHAPTER 1

Order

My dad, Loy Sartin, couldn't stay put. He'd move us from one farm to the next, chasing work. Every spring, when the fields started greening, he'd get that restless look. "Time to go," he'd say, and my mother, Tessie, would start packing, her quiet sigh speaking volumes.

I'd watch Dad as he loaded up our car, his tall, trim frame moving with purpose. The sun would catch his dark hair, peppered with streaks of gray, and for a moment, I'd see glimpses of the young Army soldier he once was.

Mother was a beacon of stability in our ever-shifting world. Her poofy hair, always neatly styled, bounced with each step she took. High cheekbones gave her face an elegant look, but it was her smile that truly defined her. Even in the chaos of packing and moving, that smile seemed almost permanent, as if it were her natural state of being.

Our family rolled across state lines like tumbleweeds. Kansas winds, California sun, Illinois cornfields—we saw it all. By fifth grade, I'd been to five different schools, always the new girl, always starting over.

That year on the Illinois turkey farm sticks in my mind. I was eight, eye-level with those mean birds. They'd strut around, feathers puffed, gobbling threats. One look from me and they'd charge, a feathered army with sharp beaks. I'd run screaming, heart pounding.

Being the oldest girl meant growing up fast. While other girls cuddled dolls, I juggled real babies. I changed diapers standing on tiptoes, reaching across the counter. Bath time was a production—lining up squirming siblings, scrubbing behind ears, mediating splash fights. At night, I'd perch on the edge of a bed, reading stories until little eyes drooped shut.

Sometimes, on warm afternoons after chores, I'd stand on our front steps. Neighborhood kids would run by, jump ropes slapping the sidewalk, their laughter floating on the breeze. For a moment, I'd imagine joining them, feeling the rope's rhythm, sharing whispered secrets.

But then a little voice would call from inside. "Judy, I'm hungry!" or "Help me with my spelling!" I'd turn away from the street, back to my family. This was my place, where small hands reached for me and young eyes looked up to me. It wasn't the childhood I'd dreamed of, but it was mine.

When I was twelve, we finally settled in Seymour, Missouri. The joy of staying put almost made up for our house's lack of running water. Each day, my brother Larry and I trudged downhill to the old pump. Its handle creaked with each stroke. On our return home, our lungs burned, and our small shoulders ached under the weight of the buckets. We were careful not to slosh over the sides. By the third trip, my arms felt like lead, fingers cramping around the handle. Once the porch barrel was full, I'd rush inside to help Mother start dinner.

Each evening I'd stand at the sink, soap suds up to my elbows, while a pot simmered on the stove. My schoolbooks lay untouched as I folded another load of laundry. These tasks filled my hours, but I felt a quiet pride in keeping our home running.

Mother was my most important teacher, and our home was her classroom. "Judy," she'd instruct, eyes sharp but kind, "dust first, then vacuum. Otherwise, you're just dirtying the floor all over again!" Her sink never held a dirty dish, her floors gleamed, and even the town preacher removed his shoes at our doorstep.

I'd watch my mother's hands, learning from every movement. She'd smooth wrinkles from sheets, her fingers creasing perfect folds. "No sitting on made beds," she'd warn with a smile. "You'll leave butt prints!"

Mother wielded her broom and dustpan like weapons against uncertainty. I saw it in her eyes as she surveyed our tidy rooms—satisfaction, pride, a sense of order in our chaotic lives. Her quiet strength showed in every polished surface and neatly arranged drawer.

Side by side at the ironing board or elbow-deep in dishwater, my Mother and I forged a bond stronger than blood. These endless chores became our shared language. In her patient teachings and gentle corrections, I found pieces of myself—a caretaker, a nurturer, a woman who could face life's messes head-on.

My grandparents' farms were treasure troves of childhood memories, each offering its own unique respite from my responsibilities at home.

On my maternal grandparents' farm, working the fields with Grandpa gave me a sense of peace I rarely found elsewhere. I'll never forget the day he let me drive the tractor. I was a scrawny thing, barely able to peek over the steering wheel. Grandpa hoisted me onto the metal seat, his calloused hands gentle. "Take her around the field," he said. When I hesitated, he gave me a reassuring smile. "You've got this, Judy Ann. Nice and easy now."

The engine's roar vibrated through me as I gripped the wheel, knuckles white. My first attempt was less than graceful—a jolt forward followed by a panicked stomp on the brake. Grandpa just chuckled. "Give her a little gas," he coached. The second try went smoother. As I guided the tractor around the field's edge, Grandpa's proud gaze warmed me more than the summer sun. In that moment, I felt unstoppable.

Those farm days were precious, though not without mishaps. Once, I devoured what I thought was a box of chocolates, only to discover they were Grandma's laxatives. When I confessed to Grandpa, red-faced with embarrassment, he just grinned. "I reckon you learned your lesson," he said, his eyes twinkling with amusement. Unlike my parents, Grandpa didn't scold me. He knew that some lessons are best learned the hard way.

My paternal grandparents' farm was a different kind of haven. These trips were mine alone—no siblings tagging along. It was my chance to escape household duties and bask in Grandma's undivided attention. Her hands, rough from years of farm work, were gentler than any I'd known. In a world that often felt shaky, the days on her farm were solid ground.

Each morning, we'd rise with the sun to gather eggs. Grandma would hold me up, steadying me as I reached for those blue-green treasures. The henhouse air was thick with the scent of straw and feathers, the hens grumbling at our intrusion with soft clucks and peeps. Back in the kitchen, I'd carry the egg basket like it held the crown jewels, watching my step. Then we'd whip up breakfast fit for royalty—fluffy omelets oozing cheese, and pancakes bursting with fresh-picked blackberries.

Those blackberry-picking excursions are etched in my memory. Grandma would pack a simple picnic—fresh biscuits and well water in tin cups. Finding a blackberry bush was like discovering buried treasure. I'd stuff my mouth until juice stained my chin purple, the thorns' scratches a small price to pay. Grandma would just smile, steadily filling her own bucket while I gorged.

Blackberry season also meant hauling out the old ice cream maker. Grandma and I would take turns cranking that metal bucket, our laughter mixing with the burn in our arms. Licking the rich purple custard from the paddle was my reward. Those bowls of homemade blackberry ice cream on sweltering afternoons tasted like pure summer joy.

I knew both sets of grandparents treasured spending time together as much as I did. Whether it was Grandpa's proud smile as I drove the tractor or Grandma's contented humming as we worked, their love was a constant. At day's end, curled up in Grandma's feather bed or listening to Grandpa's quiet wisdom, I'd drift off to sleep, my heart full and satisfied.

As summer faded, I returned home, the warmth of my grandparents' love tucked away like a hidden treasure. Life fell back into its familiar rhythm of chores and homemaking.

But sometimes, joy broke through the routine. One day, Mother surprised us with a trip to Seymour's Appleseed Festival. The usually quiet town square buzzed with laughter and chatter, transformed into a bustling carnival.

We wandered through the crowd, the sweet taste of fudge on our tongues, when an announcer's voice cut through the noise. "The greased pig contest is about to begin!" This bizarre rural tradition involved chasing an oil-slicked pig in a pen.

Volunteers soon discovered how difficult that was. The pig, likely questioning its life choices, became a slippery escape artist, dodging grasping hands with ease.

My brother Larry saw a worthy challenge. "Come on, Judy!" he yelled, tugging my arm. "We're gonna catch that pig!"

What followed was mayhem. As the crowd roared with laughter, people lunged and scrambled after the elusive animal. Larry and I slipped and stumbled, our faces smeared with dirt. Just when I thought we'd lost, Larry let out a triumphant yell and threw himself onto the pig. I piled on top, clinging to the squealing creature as our competitors tried to pry it away.

The announcer's voice boomed: "We have our winners!" Larry and I beamed as we took our prize home, naming him Oink Oink and building him a cozy pen. We sneaked him treats and scratched behind his ears, our new pet quickly becoming part of the family.

Weeks later, Oink Oink had vanished. We searched everywhere, our voices growing hoarse from calling his name. Finally, Mother sat us down, her face unreadable.

"Don't look for Oink Oink anymore," she said softly, then paused. "We had to eat him."

The words hit like a punch to the gut: Our beloved pet had become last week's barbecue.

Mother had a gift for comfort, finding the right words even in our shared pain. Her strength amazed me, offering love despite our hardships. She worked hard to make our house feel normal. Fresh cookies and folded towels were her attempt at order. But beneath this tidy surface, darkness lurked.

At night, a different scene unfolded. Screams, slaps, and breaking glass filled our home. Dad's voice, loud and scary, always came with the violence.

We all walked on eggshells around him. A slammed door could mean a slap. Spilled milk at dinner might spark his anger. A toy left out could become a weapon. So we moved around our home like ghosts. Before entering a room, we'd pause, listening for Dad's heavy breathing or the clink of a bottle. At night, I'd lie awake, tense, waiting for the next outburst.

Mother took the worst of it, her skin marked by Dad's fists and boots. As the violence grew, I became a target too. I stayed quiet, never flinching or crying out. Each time was worse. Once, a hit to my head left my ear ringing. When I touched it, confused by the strange sensation, my fingers came away wet with blood.

When Dad's temper flared, I'd rush my siblings into closets or under beds. If there was no time to hide, I'd stand in front of them, my arms spread wide. As the eldest sister, I thought my skin could take it better. But I couldn't stop every hit.

After the storm passed, I'd check their small bodies. My fingers would gently probe for bruises, pressing ice to swollen skin. "Shh, it's okay now," I'd whisper, even as my own ribs ached.

After nights filled with shouting and the sound of fists on flesh, I'd tiptoe to my parents' room. My small hands would tremble as I placed a folded note on Dad's pillow. "I'm sorry for making you mad," I'd write in wobbly letters. I never knew if he read them.

Even as bruises bloomed on my skin, a part of me still

yearned for his approval. I'd watch him in quiet moments—tossing apples in the fall or whistling a familiar hymn—and glimpse the father I remembered.

At school, teachers' eyes would linger on the marks on my arms and neck. Their brows would furrow, but they always looked away. Once, I almost told a friend, the words bubbling up in my throat. But I swallowed them back, along with my tears.

I'd pray each night, my fingers clasped so tight they'd turn white. "Please," I'd whisper to the darkness, "bring back my real dad." In the morning, I'd try again—offering a smile, a kind word, convinced that if I loved him enough, he'd change.

One night, when I was ten, a whimper woke me up. At the bottom of the stairs lay Mother, clutching her belly, tears streaming down her face.

Blood pooled beneath her.

"The baby..." she whispered, her voice barely audible. "The baby..."

Dad stood over her, his face pale and unfamiliar. "Oh God, oh God. I'm sorry. I don't...I didn't mean to..." he stammered.

But his fists had already done their work. His rage had robbed their unborn child of life. At the hospital, doctors spoke in hushed tones. Police came with notepads, but Mother shook her head. "A terrible accident," she murmured, her eyes downcast.

For months after, Mother drifted through our house like

a shadow. When she emerged from the bedroom, her eyes were vacant. At ten, I couldn't grasp the weight of losing a child nor understand how long that grief might linger.

At eleven, I came home to a scene that would haunt me for years. Dad lay on the kitchen floor, wrists slashed, blood seeping into the worn linoleum.

I froze in the doorway, my schoolbag slipping from my numb fingers. Only the approaching wail of sirens jolted me into action. I dropped to my knees beside Dad, pressing dish towels to his wounds with trembling hands. His clouded eyes met mine, unfocused and distant.

"Sins...forgiveness..." Dad mumbled. I clung to him, my voice cracking as I begged him to hold on.

When the ambulance came, I stepped back, my dress stained crimson. The paramedics rushed in, their voices urgent but calm. As they whisked Dad away, I stood shaking, my mind struggling to make sense of what I'd seen.

I overheard whispers that revealed the truth: Mother had found a spark of courage and told Dad she was leaving. His response was to turn his violence on himself.

In the hospital, Mother barely left Dad's side. Her face, etched with guilt and fear, told its own story. The brave woman who had tried to break free was gone. When we returned home, life fell back into its old, uncomfortable patterns.

But something had shifted. When I looked at Dad now, I saw not just the man who had hurt us, but someone capable of hurting himself. The kitchen floor had been scrubbed clean, but the memory of that day lingered, a stain that wouldn't fade.

At night, I'd lie awake, replaying the scene in my mind. The man I'd feared, the father I'd longed for, and the broken figure on our kitchen floor blurred together. I was left with questions that had no easy answers, forced to see our family—and the world—through different eyes.

CHAPTER 2

Secrets

The Sartin family perfected the art of secrecy. Mother would limp to the grocery store, forcing a smile. "Missed a step," she'd explain, her eyes darting away from concerned looks.

As the oldest girl, I became the star performer in our show of normalcy. I'd stand in front of the mirror, practicing how to hide my winces, how to explain away the bruises. "I fell," I'd rehearse, or "I'm just clumsy."

Night after night, I'd stare at the ceiling, my mind a carousel of questions. *What had I done wrong? Why did Dad's fists find me? Why did Mother cry?* If I could just be better, maybe the storms would pass. These thoughts were my lullaby, guilt my constant companion.

Even summers at Grandpa's farm, meant to be an escape, became another stage for secrets. The smell of hay promised freedom, but danger lurked. A relative, his breath hot on my neck, whispered about teaching me to ride horses.

His hands wandered where they shouldn't. I learned to float above myself, watching from far away as it happened.

By ten, I'd mastered hiding these occurrences from the family. Each one was a brick in the wall I built around myself. In the mirror, a girl with hollow eyes stared back. She knew things no child should, felt pains that had no name.

In the Sartin family, we didn't just keep secrets—we became them. And I was becoming the biggest secret of all.

The summer before my freshman year of high school, Mother and Dad found religion. This wasn't the gentle faith of hymns and potlucks. The Pentecostal pastor's words crackled like lightning, warnings of hellfire and damnation. Every sermon promised to fix our broken lives, if only we followed the rules.

I watched, puzzled, as my parents embraced this new world. It was as if they thought these strict beliefs could erase our family's dark secrets. The irony wasn't lost on me—seeking salvation in a place that demanded even more hiding, more pretending.

Overnight, our house transformed into a fun-free zone. TV vanished, radio fell silent. Apparently, Elvis and *I Love Lucy* were our express tickets to damnation. Our closets endured a holy purge too. Anything remotely eye-catching was banished. We girls became walking billboards of modesty, our hair uncut, our limbs hidden.

Summer brought a special kind of torture. While other

kids splashed in pools and chased ice cream trucks, I sweltered in bulky dresses. Sundays turned into otherworldly spectacles, with adults babbling away in "tongues" while we kids daydreamed about freedom and breezy outfits.

Yet underneath all that holiness, our old secrets were still festering like open wounds. We'd go to church, pray till our knees ached, and follow every edict like our eternal souls depended on it. But even as we prayed louder and longer, familiar sounds haunted our nights—the thud of a fist, muffled sobs.

Religion became just our family's newest act, another way to duck and weave around the pain we were carrying. And so, we kept going, outwardly righteous and inwardly broken, chasing salvation that always seemed just out of reach.

By some miracle, we stayed put in Missouri long enough for me to do all four years at one high school. We moved to Springfield, where I was able to attend Parkview High School. It was the crown jewel of local education, where doctors' and lawyers' kids went. The girls walked through the halls wearing the latest styles, with silk scarves around their shoulders and pleated skirts cut daringly above the knee.

Compared to them, I looked straight out of *Little House on the Prairie*, with my high-necked shirts and below-the-knee skirts. Mother played fashion police every morning, making sure not even a whisper of skin showed where it shouldn't. While other girls were finding themselves in bell-bottoms and miniskirts, I was trapped in a time capsule of curly bobs and puffy sleeves.

At night, I'd take out the fashion magazines hidden under my mattress and dive under the covers with my contraband. With a flashlight and bated breath, I'd trace the silhouettes of short dresses and the curves of mascaraed eyes, letting my imagination run wild.

By far the church's worst rule was not being allowed to date. I couldn't attend school dances or even talk to boys until I turned eighteen. So while my classmates were all aflutter about the spring formal and their latest crushes, I was at home, elbow-deep in dish soap, dreaming of a universe where being female wasn't synonymous with being dirty.

Those years were a special kind of lonely. Every morning, I'd meticulously smooth my below-the-knee-length skirt, take a deep breath, and start my pilgrimage to school. As soon as I was out of sight, I'd hike that waistband up, savoring those few precious inches of freedom. For a fleeting moment, I could pretend to be just another ordinary girl, before reluctantly unfurling my skirt back to its godly length.

It was a daily ritual, my own private rebellion. In those brief moments with my knees scandalously exposed, I wasn't Judy the Pentecostal Misfit. I was just Judy, a teenager trying to find her place in a world that seemed to spin a little faster, shine a little brighter, for everyone but me.

By my last year of high school, I was desperate for friendship, laughter, and just one normal teenage experience away from the church's watchful eyes. My salvation came in the form of Donna.

Donna was a firecracker with a smart mouth and a devil-may-care attitude that made her proper parents' hair curl. She scared me and thrilled me in equal measure.

Donna was an only child, and her wealthy parents had given her the ultimate teenage status symbol: a brand-new car. During lunch, she would sneak out to the parking lot with a few other brave souls to talk, smoke, and play loud music.

When she invited me to join them one day, I didn't hesitate. My hands shook with excitement and nerves as I got into the back seat. The air was thick with smoke. I watched, wide-eyed, as the girls passed cigarettes back and forth, blowing lazy swirls of smoke out the cracked windows.

After taking a long drag, Donna passed a cigarette to me with a daring look in her eye. "Want to try, Judy?" she said. I hesitated, knowing how harshly Mother and Dad would punish me if they ever found out. But my desire to fit in was stronger than my fear.

I held it between my fingers, trying to look as casual as the other girls. Wanting to seem cool and calm, I put it to my lips and took a deep breath, like I had seen them do. Right away, the harsh smoke burned my throat and filled my nose. I doubled over, coughing hard until my eyes watered and I thought I might throw up.

The girls laughed loudly, patting me on the back. "You'll get used to it!" Donna said. Still coughing, I passed it on, feeling embarrassed but also excited to be included in this group of mysterious, worldly girls. For the rest of lunch, I simply enjoyed their lively talk and the dizzying new feeling spreading through my body.

In the stuffy, quiet car, their bold talk of boys and gossip made my real life seem even more suffocating. I realized how much I had missed by not having friends. Though we came from different worlds, they accepted me without judgment or expectation.

One day, high on our own rebellion, we decided to skip school altogether. For Donna, it was just another Tuesday. For me, it was like jumping off a cliff without a parachute.

Huddled in Donna's kitchen, someone floated the idea of piercing our ears. The church considered piercings sacrilegious, but Donna's eyes locked onto mine, daring me to shed my holy roller skin.

The ritual was primitive and terrifying. Ice cube, needle, muffled scream, repeat. I watched, transfixed, as the first girl's earlobe surrendered to the needle, a bead of blood welling up like a tiny, forbidden ruby.

Donna walked over and held out her open hand. In it was a shiny needle, looking dangerous. The ice cube was melting in my sweaty hand as I stood on the edge of a decision.

I lifted the cube to my earlobe with shaking fingers, holding it there for as long as I could, the water running down my wrist. Another girl came over and held the needle to my ear. I flinched as the needle went in. The pain was terrible, but I didn't make a sound, afraid of being embarrassed. The bead slid into place, cool against my hot skin. Then came the next ear.

In the weeks that followed, I worried that my parents would notice, so I purposely did not wear earrings around them. I only wore them at school, and then quickly took them out on the way home to avoid detection. To keep my ears clean, I'd wash my earlobes with peroxide at school, and then store the bottle in my school locker.

Those tiny holes in my ears felt like windows to another world. It was a small act of defiance, sure, but it was mine. And in my world of suffocating rules and endless amens, that little bit of metal felt like pure, unadulterated freedom.

For years, I'd balanced between two worlds—my family's and my own. That tightrope snapped the day Assistant Pastor Joseph McClatchy offered me a ride home from my after-school job.

He pulled into an empty lot, the car engine ticking as it cooled. When he reached for a beer, my stomach knotted. What followed left me shattered. His weight pinned me down, silencing my protests. I squeezed my eyes shut, lips moving in silent prayer.

He dropped me off at home and I stumbled to our front door, my legs shaky, clothes askew.

Through hiccupping sobs, I told my parents. They marched me to the head pastor—Joseph's father.

His eyes hardened as I spoke, his frown deepening. He accused me of being under an evil influence. In his eyes, questioning a man of God was a sin worse than the act itself.

In that moment, something inside me broke. The church, once a refuge, now felt like a prison. Every rule, every hymn, every sermon suddenly rang hollow.

The next Sunday, I stared at the church's white steeple, my feet rooted to the sidewalk. Inside, voices raised in praise. I turned and walked away, leaving behind my family, my faith, my community—everything I'd ever known.

I drifted through school in a fog. Math problems blurred before my eyes, and class discussions buzzed like white noise. Friends would touch my arm, their faces creased with worry, but I barely felt it. I barely felt anything.

As June approached, just walking through the school doors felt like pushing through quicksand. A few weeks before graduation, I stopped going to school. My locker sat untouched, books collecting dust inside. No diploma meant no future—or so I thought.

My classmates rushed around buying prom dresses and yearbooks. I pulled the covers over my head, hoping to sleep forever. But the ache in my chest never eased. One day, desperate for peace, I emptied a bottle of pills into my palm and swallowed them all.

My mother found me after I'd vomited up the pills into the toilet. I'd tried to end it all, and instead, I was right back where I started: alive and miserable.

To appease my shaken parents, I went through the motions of living. But the girl they knew—their smiling, chattering Judy Ann—was gone. Words dried up in my throat, and joy became a foreign concept.

At night, drawn by pulsing beats, I found my way to a teen dance hall. Inside, I lost myself in the crowd of unknown bodies and the loud music shaking the walls.

The outside world with all its cruelty faded away. For a few hours, I could forget.

But one night, mid-twirl, a heavy hand gripped my shoulder. I turned to see Dad's face, etched with anger and hurt. Someone had told him where to find me. As he led me out, the music faded. My brief taste of freedom turned bitter, like ashes on my tongue.

CHAPTER 3

Surprise

My parents packed my bags and sent me to Aunt Wanda's in Seymour. The bus ride felt like exile; Springfield's city lights faded in the rearview mirror.

At Seymour Beauty Academy, under Aunt Wanda's watchful eye, I learned to tame wild manes into sleek styles. My hands, once restless and destructive, now moved with purpose. Scissors snipped, combs glided, and perms steamed. By day's end, my feet ached and my fingers cramped, but for the first time since McClatchy's attack, I slept without nightmares.

Seymour's quiet streets were a world away from Springfield's neon glow. No dance halls here, just the rhythmic click of sprinklers on neat lawns. Yet in this stillness, something inside me began to settle.

The salon hummed with blow-dryers and gentle gossip. Surrounded by the scent of shampoo and the warmth of dryers, I slowly pieced myself back together. It wasn't glamorous work, but it was honest. And in that honesty, I glimpsed a version of myself I hadn't seen in years—someone with a future.

I turned eighteen in Seymour—a legal adult at last. No more curfews, no more being under anyone's thumb—not my parents', not the church's, not Aunt Wanda's. The world was wide open, and I was itching to explore.

One balmy summer night, a group of us drove to the edge of town. A boy named Dylan and I wandered away from the others. When he kissed me, the tang of cheap beer and cigarettes filled my mouth, but the thrill of being wanted made me dizzy.

The magic faded fast when Dylan got rough, forcing me to the ground. Fear flooded my body—I knew I was in trouble. Just as panic set in, a boy with brown hair appeared. He yanked Dylan off me and tossed him aside.

My rescuer's voice was smooth and sweet as he introduced himself as Charlie. He drove me home, a perfect gentleman, his calm demeanor soothing my rattled nerves.

In the weeks that followed, Charlie and I spent long evenings talking in my driveway. His motorcycle gleamed under the streetlights, matching his rugged charm. I'd never met anyone so self-assured, so worldly.

Our romance unfolded in a flurry of nighttime drives and stolen moments. Charlie's presence made my head spin in ways I'd never experienced. I was intoxicated, falling headlong into young love.

Charlie's motorcycle was his most prized possession. He would spend hours fixing and polishing it, fussing over the machine as if it were his firstborn child. I was both thrilled and intimidated by it.

One sunny afternoon, Charlie tossed me the keys with a playful grin. "Want to take her for a ride?"

I hesitated, licking my dry lips. "Sure!" I said. I was trying to hide the fact that I had no idea how to ride a motorcycle.

Heart pounding, I carefully got on the vibrating seat. I wobbled forward a few feet before stalling out, my cheeks burning. But Charlie just laughed kindly, steadying me with a light hand until I got my balance back.

"All right, let's see you take her around the block real slow now," he instructed. I nodded, my teeth clenched in concentration. The engine roared to life once more beneath me. I eased forward, the bike humming as houses and trees slid past in a thrilling blur.

I sped up, determined to impress Charlie. It was too late before I noticed the stop sign at the corner. "The brake! Which one's the brake?" I screeched, flying past Charlie's suddenly pale face.

My fingers scrambled over unfamiliar levers. The bike sputtered and tipped, dumping me unceremoniously into a ditch.

Charlie sprinted over, his eyes darting between me and his fallen bike. "You little liar!" he growled, hauling me up. "You could've gotten yourself killed!"

I braced for more, but Charlie's anger melted into laughter. Despite my stinging palms and bruised pride, I found myself grinning back. In his eyes, I saw a new respect—and that was worth all the scrapes in the world.

The church's teachings about purity echoed in my ears, but Charlie's touch drowned them out. He was my first in every way—first boyfriend, first lover. Never having dated before, each new experience left me dizzy and craving more.

We stole moments in the shadows, our racing hearts drowning out the warnings of eternal damnation that had been drilled into us. The secrecy only intensified our desires. We convinced ourselves that love this strong couldn't be wrong, even as guilt gnawed at the edges of our consciences.

Charlie awakened a part of me I hadn't known existed. When we were together, the world fell away. Weeks blurred into months. Our boldness grew, along with our disregard for consequences. We were invincible, or so we thought, drunk on young love and the thrill of rebellion.

But reality has a way of shattering illusions. The day I told Charlie about the baby, I watched panic flash in his eyes, mirroring my own fear. This wasn't just youthful fun anymore—we'd created something that threatened to upend both our lives.

In that moment, childhood ended abruptly. We found ourselves teetering on the edge of a very adult problem, the ground crumbling beneath our feet.

My voice cracked as I mumbled the word *pregnant* in front of my parents. For a moment, silence reigned.

Then, chaos erupted. Mother crumpled onto the couch, her sobs filling the room. Dad's face flushed red, his anger building like a storm.

"I'd rather see that boy dead than have you disgraced under my roof!" he bellowed, each word louder than the last.

Dad strode to where he kept his shotgun. My heart leapt to my throat. Mother finally stepped between us, her voice sharp.

"She'll marry him," she declared, eyes locked on mine. "You'll have your first child in seven months. We'll tell everyone it's premature. No one needs to know the truth."

The word *truth* hung in the air like smoke. This wasn't a suggestion—it was a command.

Before I could process what was happening, a simple gold band adorned my finger, and Charlie and I were unpacking boxes in his sister's spare room. Just weeks ago, we were stealing kisses. Now, we were engaged to be husband and wife.

At night I'd lie awake, listening to Charlie's steady breathing beside me. I stared at the unfamiliar walls, my mind reeling. We were barely more than children ourselves—how were we supposed to be parents?

On my wedding day, I woke with a heavy heart, eyes puffy from another night of tears. At eighteen, I was trading my dreams for a life I hadn't chosen.

The house buzzed with activity. Amid the chaos, my six-year-old brother Jamie's excitement was infectious. He'd been practicing his ring bearer walk for weeks, navy suit pressed and waiting.

That morning, I found Jamie in the bathroom, a proud grin splitting his face. My heart stopped. He'd taken a razor to his soft brown hair, carving a crooked stripe down the center of his head.

"Jamie, what have you done?!" I gasped. He beamed up at me, proud as could be.

"I cut my hair! Do you like it?" he asked, grinning.

My shouts brought Mother running. She went pale at the sight of her little ring bearer's ruined hair. "*James Edward,* what did you do?!" she yelled.

"I just fixed my hair!" he replied, unfazed by the commotion.

As Jamie marched solemnly down the aisle, chin high, I cracked my only smile of the day. Those wedding photos would be something to see.

In that moment, watching my little brother's crooked haircut bobbing down the aisle, I felt a flicker of lightness. Even on this day of endings and uncertain beginnings, life found a way to surprise me.

Early on in our courtship, Charlie loved that an older girl had chosen him. But marriage and impending fatherhood hit him like a bucket of cold water. Suddenly, we faced a life of responsibilities neither of us was ready for.

When Charlie talked about quitting school, I refused to

let him. "One of us needs that diploma," I said, my hand resting on my bump. "And it won't be me."

While Charlie slept late and charmed his way through his senior year, I waddled between tables as a waitress. The apron barely covered my growing stomach as I balanced trays and dodged customers' curious glances.

Night after night, I'd drag myself home, feet swollen, back aching. The apartment would be empty. Sometimes I'd spot a smudge of lipstick on Charlie's collar or catch a whiff of unfamiliar perfume. But I'd shake my head, banishing the thoughts. Surely, he wouldn't...

Mother's voice echoed in my head: "Marriage is forever." I'd seen her weather Dad's storms for years. No one in our family divorced. It just wasn't done.

So I swallowed Charlie's excuses like bitter pills. It was easier to believe the lies than face the truth.

The first time Charlie's palm connected with my cheek, I blinked in shock. "It was an accident," I told myself. But soon, the sting of his hand became as familiar as his touch once was.

"Where were you?" I'd ask when he stumbled in late. His eyes, once warm, now turned to ice. The answering slap echoed in our small apartment. I learned to swallow my questions along with my pride.

To Charlie, I was an anchor weighing him down. The baby growing inside me? Just another chain. One night, after a heated argument, he shoved me. I tumbled down the stairs, my hands instinctively cradling my swollen belly.

As I lay there, pain radiating through me, I prayed the baby was okay. But a part of me feared Charlie might try again.

As my due date approached, Charlie's drinking worsened. He'd stumble home reeking of booze or vanish for days. In those final weeks of pregnancy, I'd drive aimlessly through town, searching for his familiar silhouette in every bar window. "If I could just talk to him," I'd think, "maybe we could fix this." But I always ended up back home, alone in the dark, tears staining my pillow.

One balmy evening at the carnival, I spotted a head of hair I'd know anywhere, peeking above a parked convertible. Charlie's friends materialized, trying to block my path. But I pushed past them, my heart in my throat.

There was Charlie, all right. And there was a wide-eyed brunette, hastily tugging her dress back into place.

In that moment, the truth I'd been avoiding hit me hard: Charlie never loved me. He'd only loved the thrill of pursuit. Now, with a baby on the way and a ring on my finger, I was old news. And I was utterly alone.

The first contraction hit me at home, when I was by myself, no Charlie in sight.

I called my mother, and her car pulled up minutes later. "Breathe, honey," she murmured, smoothing my hair as we sped to the hospital.

In the delivery room, between waves of pain, my eyes darted to the door. Any moment now, I thought, Charlie would burst in, breathless and excited. But the chair beside me remained empty as Angel's first cry filled the air.

Mother went home to fetch clothes for me and the baby. What she found shocked her: beer bottles everywhere, overflowing ashtrays, and Charlie passed out next to two strange women.

She returned to the hospital, her lips pressed into a thin line. "You're staying with me until you're back on your feet." Her tone left no room for argument.

A week later, Charlie showed up at Mother's doorstep. His arms were full of diapers and formula, his smile wide and apologetic. "I'm sorry," he cooed, eyes fixed on Angel. "I get it now. I know what's important."

I watched him cradle our daughter, his fingers gentle as he traced her tiny features. For a moment, I let myself hope. Maybe fatherhood had changed him. Maybe this time would be different.

Against my better judgment, against the memory of empty promises and stinging slaps, I nodded. "Okay," I whispered, "one more chance."

This time would be different. It had to be. Right?

My hope for change was short-lived. As weeks turned to months, and months to years, Charlie's true colors bled through his charming façade.

Charlie's handsome face hid a cruel heart, and alcohol was the key that unleashed it. Sober, he'd reminisce about our early days, all sweet words and gentle touches. But when he drank, a monster emerged.

Nights were the hardest. I'd sit in the dim light of our living room, ears straining for the sound of his car. The front door would slam, and the house would hold its breath.

Some nights he was just confused, stumbling and slurring. Other nights, rage radiated from him like heat. But always, always, his eyes were bloodshot and unfocused.

Nine years after Angel, I was pregnant again. I dared to hope this might be the turning point—that, with a second baby on the way, Charlie would become the father and husband he promised he could be. We had our good moments, the bits of peace between the fighting. We'd go to the lake every weekend, enjoying the time together as a family. But then Charlie would drink, and the joy evaporated.

In quiet moments, I'd imagine grabbing Angel and running, starting fresh in some nameless town where Charlie couldn't find us. I had a job, a little money saved. But years of fists and cruel words had worn me down. Leaving felt as impossible as outrunning a tornado.

After each explosion of violence came the calm. Charlie would apologize, his voice thick with tears, showering me with affection. In these moments, I'd glimpse the man I thought I'd married, and a traitorous hope would flicker to life.

But inevitably, tension would build again. I'd see it in the set of his jaw, the clench of his fists. Then would come the storm of violence, followed by another round of apologies. This cycle wrapped around me like chains, binding me with a mix of fear, misplaced love, and false hope.

I knew how it looked from the outside. Why didn't she just leave? But walking out that door meant more than just packing a bag. It meant untangling years of manipulation, of being told I was worthless, that no one else would want me. Trying to leave felt like being trapped in a maze where every turn led back to the start.

So I pushed thoughts of escape deep down, focusing instead on shielding my children from the worst of it. I convinced myself that enduring was the only option. And endure I did, through bruised skin, shattered trust, and endless nights of dread.

Just after my third wedding anniversary, Mother's words hit me like a thunderbolt: "I'm leaving your father." Though long overdue, her decision left me reeling.

It began with a broken TV and a repairman named Larry. He arrived with a toolbox and left with Mother's heart. Larry was everything Dad wasn't—gentle hands, soft voice, kind eyes. We started calling him Teddy Bear. Watching them together, I saw Mother smile in a way I'd forgotten she could.

When Mother confided her plan to leave, a storm brewed inside me. The church's teachings echoed in my head: "Marriage is sacred. A wife's duty is to her husband, always." For three years, I'd lived by those words, enduring Charlie's fists and fury, believing it was God's will.

I understood Mother's yearning for peace after years of pain. But another voice, shaped by Sunday sermons and Bible studies, whispered "sinner" in my ear. Leaving seemed as foreign as flying. In my tangled thoughts, it felt more like betrayal than self-preservation.

Yet, beneath the confusion and guilt, a quiet wish took root: I wanted Mother to be happy. This simple desire shook the foundation of everything I thought I knew about love and duty.

Before making it final, Mother and Dad sought our minister's advice. His words were familiar: "Marriage is forever. You must endure." But I saw a new resolve in Mother's eyes. She'd made her choice long ago, in moments of quiet desperation I'd never witnessed.

Mother divorced Dad and married Larry. She chose love and kindness over religion and duty. And seeing them together—Larry's gentle touch, Mother's radiant smile—I couldn't deny the rightness of it.

With Mother gone, I invited Dad to live with Charlie and me. I hoped caring for him might mend our broken bond. But he arrived with suitcases full of bitterness, his demons amplified by the bottle. Even Charlie tried to help, organizing hunting trips and card games. Yet our home remained shrouded in a fog of resentment and barely contained violence, as thick and suffocating as ever.

CHAPTER 4

Thunderbird

The Royals game ran late due to rain. When I finally got home, Charlie's breath reeked of whiskey.

"Why are you home so late?!" he barked.

"The game had a rain delay," I responded. "I'm sorry."

"I don't believe you!" he yelled. "Where the hell were you?!"

Before I could explain further, his fist connected with my jaw. The next thing I knew, I was flying through our glass front door.

I hit the porch hard, shards of glass biting into my skin. Warm blood seeped through my blouse. Then I heard it—Angel's scream. She ran past me as I tried to crawl toward her. She bolted into the night, so I rushed to my feet, caught up to her, and pulled her into my arms. We rushed to the phone to call 911. The dispatcher's calm voice promised help.

Wrapping ourselves in a blanket, we sat on the front steps, waiting for the police. Every minute felt like an hour. Where were the sirens?

Finally, blue lights appeared. Two officers sauntered up, their relaxed demeanor vanishing when they saw my bloodstained blanket. They asked questions, examined my cuts. Then the older one delivered words that struck harder than any of Charlie's blows:

"There's nothing we can do, ma'am. We'll tell him to leave until he sobers up. We can't arrest him."

And just like that, they left. I watched their taillights fade, feeling utterly abandoned. I wanted to scream that Charlie would kill me, but I swallowed the words. What good would it have done? No help was coming. I was on my own.

I crept back inside, relieved to find Charlie passed out on the couch. As I cleaned my wounds, each sting of antiseptic reminded me of this night—the shattering glass, Angel's scream, her terrified escape. It was burned into my memory, a turning point I could never forget.

It didn't happen right away, but a seed was planted that night. A small voice whispered: I deserved better. I was worth fighting for, even if I had to do the fighting myself.

In June 1980, I signed the divorce papers with shaking hands. Charlie packed his bags, leaving me with the kids and a hollow sense of victory. He was free to drown himself in booze and women, while I navigated single parenthood.

I thought the worst was behind me. I was wrong.

The first sign of trouble was a door left ajar when I knew I'd locked it. Inside, the scent of Charlie's cologne mingled with the stale smell of beer. My clothes lay in tatters on the bedroom floor, my shoes sliced to ribbons.

From then on, coming home became a game of Russian roulette. Would today be the day I found him waiting for me, drunk and vengeful? The peace I'd hoped for evaporated, replaced by constant dread.

I was unraveling faster than I could stitch myself back together. Years of flinching at sudden movements, of walking on eggshells, had left me raw. Now, watching my son Chip play alone, I was crushed by guilt. What kind of mother deprives her son of a father?

One September evening, the weight became too much. I found myself sitting on the cold bathroom tile, a bottle of pills in my hand. I don't remember deciding to do it. I just remember the mechanical motion of hand to mouth, swallowing until the bottle was empty. Then, I waited.

I woke to the harsh glare of hospital lights, disoriented and alive. The doctor's words filtered through slowly: Charlie had found me. He'd called 911. The neighbors had the kids until my parents could arrive.

As awareness crept back, so did the tears. I wasn't sure if I was crying from relief or disappointment. I was alive, but the thought of facing another day felt insurmountable. Yet the idea of trying again...I didn't have it in me. I was trapped in a life I didn't want, but couldn't seem to escape.

For two weeks, I sat in the psych ward, my hospital gown a stark reminder of how far I'd fallen. The psychiatrist, a kind-faced man, called it a breakdown.

"You need space from the trauma," he said softly. "To

mend your mind." His eyes crinkled as he suggested, "Perhaps a fresh start near family would help."

His words were like a small flame in the darkness. Slowly, they thawed the ice around my heart. This doctor saw worth in me when I couldn't see it in myself. I owe him everything.

When my mother came to visit, her eyes widened at the sight of me in the ward, and suddenly I was her little girl again. She reached out, smoothing my hair like she used to when I was sick.

"Come back to Springfield with us," she said. "Just until you get on your feet."

In that moment, I saw a glimmer of a future. My kids needed their mother—not this hollow shell, but the real me, alive and fighting.

The day I checked out, Mother and my stepdad were waiting. We drove straight to my old house, the air thick with urgency. Angel and Chip, twelve and three, watched wide-eyed as we packed, their childhood home disappearing into boxes.

We grabbed only what we needed. Charlie's presence lingered in every room. I was itching to escape, even if it meant starting from scratch.

Soon we were headed 170 miles south to Springfield. As familiar landmarks faded in the rearview mirror, Mother reached back to grip my hand. My marriage was over, I'd lost myself for a while, but now I was coming home under her wing.

We pulled up to my parents' place as the sun was setting. That first night, I lay in bed, breathing in the unfamiliar comfort. The kids were asleep in the next room, their soft snores a lullaby of normalcy.

Tomorrow would bring decisions and practicalities. But that night, I savored the goodness around me—the safety of family, the love of my parents, my babies sleeping soundly nearby. Here, we were untouchable.

"No more depending on men," I told myself. "This time, you stand on your own two feet."

My first order of business: find a house and a job. The house would have to wait, but the job? That came from a familiar source.

The bell above the door chimed as I stepped into Tess's Wig and Beauty, my mother's salon. She'd owned it for years, and she was deeply proud of it. Wigs were big business then; Mother had even sold to Dolly Parton.

When I walked in, the familiar scent of hairspray and shampoo hit me, along with a wave of memories. I'd worked here on weekends when Charlie and I would come down to visit. But this was different. This wasn't about earning money for the movies or new shoes. This was survival.

"Ready to start?" Mother asked, handing me a smock. Her eyes shone with a mix of pride and concern.

I tied the smock around my waist, noting how it settled over my hips differently now. I wasn't a carefree girl anymore, but a mother of two with everything to prove.

The work was harder than I remembered. My feet ached at the end of each day, and my hands were tired from the repetition of washing and styling. But every time I handed a woman a mirror and saw her face light up at her reflection, I felt a spark of something I hadn't felt in years: pride.

Each paycheck felt like a victory. It wasn't much, but it was mine. Earned by my hands, my skills. I'd come home exhausted, collapsing onto the couch at my parents' house, but with a satisfied smile.

"You're doing great," my stepdad would say, handing me a cup of coffee as I kicked off my shoes.

The kids would pile onto my lap, chattering about their day. For the first time in years, I felt... worthy. Loved.

One night, as I was putting the kids to bed, Mother sat down beside me. "You know," she said, her voice soft, "I battled my own demons once upon a time." She squeezed my hand. "Keep fighting, Judy Ann. You're stronger than you know."

The hum of the tanning booth faded as I stepped out, wrapping myself in a towel. That's when I overheard the owner talking.

"Yeah, I'm thinking of selling the place," he said, his voice tinged with weariness. "It's time for a change."

My ears perked up, and my heart began to race. A tanning salon for sale? I knew nothing about running such a business, but after everything I'd been through, what was one more challenge?

That night, I paced my parents' living room, the idea refusing to let go.

"I don't know the first thing about running a business," I muttered, running my fingers through my hair.

"Neither did I when I started," Mother replied, her eyes twinkling. "Sometimes you just have to trust your gut."

Soon I signed the papers, my hand trembling slightly as I wrote the check. I'd poured nearly every penny I had into this gamble.

The first months were a whirlwind. I juggled manuals for tanning beds, pored over permit applications, and deciphered health regulations. More than once, I found myself slumped over the reception desk, wondering what I'd gotten myself into.

But slowly, things began to click. Tanning was just becoming popular, and we added massages and body wraps to our offerings, expanding our client base. I discovered I had a knack for arranging displays, making the tiny spa look chic and inviting. I was aggressive with outreach, making contacts with local car dealerships, the nearby universities, any business that might want to partner up.

My sales pitch improved with each customer. "First time?" I'd ask new arrivals with a smile. "Let me show you our package deals."

The salon's location, nestled beside a towering office building, proved to be a gold mine. Suited professionals streamed in, chasing that successful glow.

"Got a big presentation tomorrow," one regular confided. "Need to look my best."

Their drive was contagious. I started seeing my salon through their eyes—not just a place to tan, but a stepping stone to success. I poured every profit back into the business, upgrading equipment and redecorating.

I approached the Miss Missouri pageant to sponsor us— and to my amazement, they said yes.

I still remember hanging up the phone with them and catching my reflection in the mirror. The woman staring back at me stood tall, confident. For the first time in years, I recognized myself.

Springfield felt like a fresh canvas, waiting for me to paint my life anew. For the first time, I could choose—my friends, my community, even my clothes. No one's judgment mattered except my own.

Day by day, color seeped back into my world. Laughter bubbled up more freely without Charlie's looming presence. As my salon thrived, I rediscovered parts of myself long buried—mother, friend, entrepreneur.

To celebrate this rebirth, I bought a sleek silver Ford Thunderbird. The vanity plate read MI TURN, a nod to Diana Ross's anthem of independence, "It's My Turn." Cruising down Main Street, I cranked up the volume: "And now it's my turn, To try and find my way, And if I should get lost, At least I'll own today."

The lyrics washed over me, each word a balm to my battered spirit. I belted out the chorus, my voice growing stronger with each line. Life, for once, seemed to be on my side. Hard work rebuilt my confidence, one small victory at a time. Money was tight, but my newfound skills kept the salon afloat. I had come too far to stumble now.

Single motherhood was a juggling act. Breaks were rare luxuries, savored in quiet sips of coffee between appointments. But watching Angel and Chip grow up without fear made every sacrifice worthwhile.

"Mom, can you help me with my math problems?" Angel would ask, her eyes bright with curiosity.

"Of course, sweetie," I'd reply, setting aside the salon's books. Our evenings were filled with homework, bedtime stories, and whispered dreams of the future.

Moving had been tough on the kids, but the stability we gained was priceless. Our days fell into a happy rhythm— school drop-offs, salon appointments, days at the park. My world orbited their innocence, and I found unexpected joy in packed lunches and math homework.

This period was humble but rich with purpose. We had carved out our slice of good in a world that had shown us its worst. But change was coming, as it always does. A series of missteps would soon teach me that freedom, like a house of cards, can topple with a single breath.

But before the fall, life was filled with promise and hard work. For a brief, beautiful moment, my small world held nothing but goodness.

CHAPTER 5

Manipulation

At the salon, I was unstoppable. My marketing ideas brought in clients by the dozens. I'd stride across the floor, confidence in every step.

But the moment a man showed romantic interest, it was like a switch flipped. The confident businesswoman disappeared, replaced by a timid girl desperate to please.

When we first moved to Springfield, I avoided dating altogether. My days were a whirlwind of school runs, client appointments, and bedtime stories. Loneliness seemed a small price to pay for peace.

But soon, things shifted. The kids became busy with school and spending time with their aunts and uncles. Suddenly, I found pockets of time I didn't know what to do with.

As life settled, I cautiously dipped my toe back in the dating pool. I kept things casual, never getting too close. Better to be careful and free than careless and trapped.

One April night, I found myself in a swanky, crowded

restaurant lounge, feeling out of place in my carefully chosen outfit. A man approached, his smile warm.

"I'm Greg," he said, extending his hand.

I accepted, my heart racing. His suit screamed success, but it was his kind eyes that drew me in. We chatted easily, and for the first time in years, I felt seen as a woman, not just a mother or business owner.

Over the next few days, Greg became a regular at the salon, always finding an excuse to stop by.

I found myself looking forward to his visits, even as a voice in the back of my mind whispered caution. It felt good to laugh with a man again, to feel that spark of connection. But I kept my guard up, determined not to lose myself again.

I felt guilty as I watched Chip play with his toys. Only three, he barely remembered Charlie. I still wondered if I was robbing him of a father figure.

"Maybe we should try again," I murmured to myself, then shook my head. The memory of Charlie's fists made no sense with these thoughts, but abuse had a way of twisting logic.

I decided to meet Charlie in Kansas City, to talk things over. When I mentioned it to Greg, he surprised me.

"I have a convention there that weekend," he said. "Why don't we drive up together? We'll get separate rooms, of course."

The meeting with Charlie was a disaster. On the drive

back, I stewed in silence, my mind a storm of conflicting emotions.

"You okay?" Greg's voice cut through my thoughts. "Need anything? I'm here as a friend if you want to talk."

His concern felt foreign after years of Charlie's indifference. Before I knew it, I was spilling everything—the abuse, the fear, the confusion.

Greg listened, his jaw tightening at the worst parts. "I'm so sorry you went through that," he said softly. "You deserved better."

After that trip, Greg asked me to dinner. Our dates became regular, and I found myself opening up to this charming stranger.

"I'm a real estate broker," he told me over dinner one night. "And a Charismatic Christian minister."

I perked up at that. It wasn't the strict Pentecostalism of my youth, but it felt familiar. I hadn't been to church since marrying Charlie, who scoffed at religion.

Greg was different from Charlie in every way. He listened when I spoke, offered comfort when I cried. For once, I felt valued.

He charmed everyone around us. My mother beamed when he brought her flowers, and Chip adored the trips to the park.

Greg painted our future in broad, colorful strokes. "We'll have a beautiful house," he'd say, his eyes sparkling. "The kids will go to the best schools. We'll travel the world."

I let myself get lost in these dreams, ignoring the nagging doubts. His tastes seemed beyond his means, his divorce dragged on, and vague "friends" often needed his help.

But I didn't ask questions. With Charlie, questions had led to fists. So I stayed silent, pushing down my need to know more about Greg's past and plans.

"You're amazing," Greg would tell me, his eyes full of admiration. "I don't know how you do it all."

His belief in me was intoxicating. I clung to this new tenderness, afraid to lose it by digging too deep or asking too many questions.

One mild June day, I came home to find suitcases in my foyer. My heart skipped a beat.

"Whose are these?" I asked, my voice echoing in the quiet house.

Greg stepped out from the living room, a sheepish smile on his face. "They're mine," he said softly.

I blinked, trying to process. "What? Why?"

Greg's smooth voice filled the space between us. "I thought we should live together, Judy. Share life's ups and downs." He moved closer, his eyes warm. "I need to take care of you and the kids."

"Greg, I've never had anyone stay with my children," I stammered. "I don't do that."

"But Judy, I love your kids. We can be one big family," he said, his grin infectious.

Images of our weekend park outings flashed through my mind—Greg playing catch with Chip, pushing Angel on the swings. It did feel like family.

After a moment of hesitation, I nodded. "Let's try it out," I heard myself say.

Within a month, any doubts I had faded. Greg became a doting father figure overnight, and our shared meals and stories felt like the family I'd always dreamed of.

That Fourth of July, we joined my extended family at my aunt's. With Greg's arm around me by the poolside, I felt hopeful about new beginnings.

As the day wore on, Greg sat absorbed in a book while I chatted with relatives in the pool. My aunt swam up to me, her voice low.

"Judy, why's he reading a book about manipulation?" she whispered. "Should we be worried about you?"

I glanced at Greg, seeing him for a moment through my aunt's eyes—an outsider studying something sinister. But the thought passed as quickly as it came.

I laughed, the sound a bit too high. "He's in real estate," I explained. "He has to know how to persuade buyers to close the sale."

My aunt seemed satisfied, but a chill ran through me despite the summer heat. If she had pressed, maybe I would have admitted the unease her words stirred in me.

Years later, I'd replay this moment. If only I'd listened to her. If only I'd asked more questions. If only I'd seen Greg for who he was.

But I didn't. I ignored the warning signs, maybe because the truth was too scary: I'd walked away from one predator... and right into the arms of another.

CHAPTER 6

Into the Night

During our trip to Kansas City, I'd gotten together with a friend, Gina, at a hotel bar. Because Greg was with me for the trip, he tagged along.

"You won't believe the size of Harry's three-carat ring," Gina gushed, her eyes sparkling. Gina had a new man in her life—Harry Klein, a flashy jewelry store owner from Springfield. She gushed about the gifts he lavished on her and their fancy trips. I soaked it all in, living vicariously through her stories.

Greg, previously disinterested, leaned in. I barely noticed his sudden interest, too caught up in Gina's world.

Weeks later, back home, I overheard Greg on the phone. His voice was low, all business. "Harry," "ring," and "three-carat..." The words drifted through the door, clear as day. A chill ran down my spine, but I pushed the worry away. Charlie had taught me well: Keep your head down. Don't ask questions.

One evening, as Greg and I sat watching TV, my phone rang. It was Gina, her voice electric with excitement.

"Judy, you'll never guess! Harry wants to meet you. He's sending his private plane to bring you to Kansas City this weekend."

I laughed, caught off guard.

"No way, Gina," I said.

"Come on, Judy," she pressed. "You never have any fun. It's all work with you."

Before I could respond, Gina passed the phone to Harry. His voice oozed charm. "Hi, Judy. I've heard so much about you," he said. "We'd love for you to visit. It'll be a great weekend."

I declined again, more firmly this time. After hanging up, I turned to Greg, expecting...what? Jealousy? Possessiveness?

"What was that about?" he asked casually.

I told him everything—the invitation, the private plane, Harry's compliments. Greg just nodded, completely unfazed.

A few days later, I was at work when the phone rang. It was Harry Klein, asking me to lunch. He wasn't subtle about his intentions. I was caught off guard but kept my cool, politely turning him down again.

Harry wasn't used to hearing no. He kept pushing, getting bolder with every try. But I held firm. No way, no how was I meeting him.

When I told Greg about it later, he shrugged it off like it was nothing. I was amazed. This modern man actually trusted me, no questions asked.

His trust felt foreign. With Charlie, a note left on my

windshield once led to accusations, threats, and eventually, bruises. Greg's faith in me was the relationship I'd always dreamed of.

And yet, a small voice in the back of my mind whispered: Is this trust, or indifference?

The salon door opened, and I looked up to see Greg walk in, flanked by two men. My stomach clenched.

"Judy, can we talk outside for a minute?" Greg's voice was casual, but his eyes were hard.

Once outside, the men huddled close, their voices low.

"Harry Klein owes me money," one of them said.

I blinked, confused. "What does that have to do with me?"

Greg's hand found my shoulder, squeezing a bit too tight. "We need you to set up a meeting with Harry. You're our in."

My mind raced back to Gina's stories, Harry's invitation. The pieces clicked into place, and I felt sick.

"I can't," I said, my voice barely a whisper. "I don't even know him."

"But he wants to know you," the other man chimed in, his smile not reaching his eyes. "That's all we need."

I shook my head, fumbling for an excuse. "I have plans. I'm busy."

Greg's face darkened. "We'll talk about this later," he muttered as the men walked away.

For days after, Greg was relentless. His words became a constant drumbeat in my ear.

"Remember how Charlie treated you?" he'd say over dinner. "I'm different. I need you, Judy. Our future depends on this."

But something deep in my gut screamed "danger." Maybe it was the memory of Charlie's manipulation, or maybe I was finally sensing the rot beneath Greg's charm. Whatever it was, I clung to it, stalling for time and praying for a way out.

Greg persisted. Each day, he'd find a new angle to approach the subject.

"It's just an old debt, Judy," he'd say, his voice smooth as silk. "Nobody's getting hurt, I promise."

When I'd shake my head, he'd lean in close, eyes pleading. "Just hear me out one more time. Please?"

Then came the bombshell.

"I need $10,000," Greg confessed one night, his eyes downcast. "It's for the divorce. If I can get that, I can leave my wife and make a home with you." He reached for my hand. "We can keep our kids together, be a real family."

My heart skipped a beat. A real family. The words echoed in my mind, stirring up long-buried dreams.

"You know I've only ever been good to you," Greg continued, his thumb tracing circles on my palm. "I love you and your kids with all I've got."

His words hit their mark. Memories of Charlie's cruelty flashed through my mind, making Greg's kindness shine even brighter.

"Think about it," he urged. "You, me, the kids. A warm house, full of love. Isn't that what you've always wanted?"

I nodded, unable to speak past the lump in my throat.

"And you can help make it happen," Greg added softly. "You'd be the one to cement our new life together."

His embarrassment about asking for money seemed so genuine. It made me want to help even more, to be the partner he needed.

With each conversation, my grip on reality loosened. Was I being selfish, putting my doubts before the man I loved? Greg seemed so sure that dealing with this Harry Klein business would secure our future.

Bit by bit, my resolve crumbled. Greg had seen right through to my deepest hurts, offering everything trauma had taught me to crave: stability, love, a whole family for my kids.

How could I say no to that?

For weeks, Greg had pleaded and cajoled, but that July evening, something shifted. The change was sudden, jarring. His friendly mask cracked, revealing something cold and hard underneath.

"Enough," he growled, cutting off my latest attempt to stall. "It's time to act."

His eyes, usually warm, turned to flint. When he spoke again, his voice was low and sharp, each word a command.

"Here's what you're gonna do," he said, brooking no

argument. "Call Harry Klein at his store. Ask to meet him there tonight." He leaned in close, his breath hot on my ear.

This wasn't a request. I felt my will crumbling, powerless to do anything but obey. His tone dredged up old fears—of Dad, the assistant pastor, Charlie—decades of terror baked into my bones.

Hands shaking, I dialed Harry's number. He answered on the second ring, his voice eager. "Judy! What a pleasant surprise."

I forced a lightness I didn't feel into my voice. "Hi Harry. I was wondering if I could stop by the store tonight?"

"Of course! I'll make sure we have privacy."

I hung up, my stomach churning. "I really, really don't want to do this," I whispered to Greg.

But he just said, "Go, Judy. It'll be fine. You have to."

Some kind of fog clouded my judgment. I went, telling myself that if Greg said it was okay, it must be.

"Do whatever he wants," Greg had ordered. "Get him worked up to go out for drinks."

In Harry's office, I followed Greg's script to the letter. We kissed, and I felt nothing but nausea. Then I made an excuse to call Greg.

"Tell Harry to follow you to Cody's Bar," Greg instructed. "Then get him to drive somewhere to meet some friends. I'll take over from there."

Greg laid out my part. After the bar, I was to lure Harry to a quiet spot outside town. There, Greg would confront him about the debt.

As I hung up, a thought wormed its way into my mind:

What was worse? Being forced into Greg's sick plan, or the nagging doubt that I could've refused if I'd been braver?

The neon sign of Cody's Bar flickered as I pulled into the parking lot, Harry's car close behind. Inside, the smoky air clung to my skin as my eyes darted around, searching for an exit. Then I saw him—Greg, hunched over a drink near the bathrooms, his face half-hidden by shadows.

"I'll be right back," I told Harry, my voice surprisingly steady. "Ladies' room."

As I passed Greg's table, he hissed, "Don't look at me! Keep walking!"

I nodded dumbly, continuing to the bathroom. When I returned, Harry was nursing his beer, oblivious to the tension thrumming through me.

"Ready to meet my friends?" I asked after we'd finished our drinks. Harry nodded eagerly, following me out to the parking lot.

Back in my Thunderbird, I gripped the steering wheel, knuckles white. For a moment, I considered driving home to my kids, leaving this nightmare behind. Suddenly, movement in the back seat caught my eye.

"Greg!" I yelped as he emerged from under a blanket. "What are you doing?"

"Just drive!" he snapped, his voice as hard as steel. I flinched, my foot instinctively pressing the gas pedal.

As streetlights gave way to the inky darkness of the countryside, my mind raced. I could turn around, end this now. I could drive straight to the police station, into safety.

Instead, I kept driving, Greg's presence a suffocating weight behind me. With each mile, we sped deeper into the night and farther from any chance of escape.

My hands trembled on the steering wheel as I veered off Greg's planned route. Suddenly, his arm snaked around my waist from the back seat. Something cold and metallic pressed against my bare thigh.

"Take this gun," Greg ordered, his voice low. "For protection."

I jerked away, my skin crawling. "No, Greg! I don't want it! What are you doing?"

Panic surged through me like an electric current. "I can't do this!" I screamed. "You said nobody would get hurt!"

In my fear and confusion, I missed the road that Greg had wanted me to turn down. I turned onto the next road, and then pulled over to the side. Harry's headlights illuminated the interior as he pulled up behind us. I saw him start to get out of his car.

Greg's hand clamped down on my arm, his fingers digging into my flesh. "Stay put," he growled.

"I need to talk to Harry!" I insisted, my voice shaking.

His grip tightened. "Don't let him near this car!"

I rolled down the window, forcing a smile. "Sorry, Harry! I'm lost. Need to turn around!"

Harry nodded, retreating to his car. As soon as his door shut, Greg's voice filled the car again.

"Turn around now. They're watching us. You have to do this, Judy."

My blood ran cold. We were being watched? The realization hit me like a punch to the gut: Greg—or whoever was out there—wouldn't hesitate to use that gun on me if I stepped out of line.

Greg steered us to a quiet country road. Harry parked behind us.

"This has to be done," Greg hissed, his eyes wild. "You're helping. Get out and pretend you've got a flat."

My legs felt like lead as I stumbled out of the car. I bent down, pretending to examine the tire. Harry's car door slammed shut as he approached.

"Need a hand?" he called out.

A flicker of movement caught my eye. I turned to see Greg, arm outstretched, a gun glinting in the moonlight. Before I could react, a crack split the night.

Pain seared across my side as the bullet grazed me before finding its mark in Harry. I lost my footing, tumbling into the ditch. Gravel bit into my palms as I pushed myself up, my dress now sticky with blood.

Dazed, I crawled back to the car, using its frame for support. Harry's voice pierced the ringing in my ears, a ragged mantra: "Oh God, oh God."

He staggered to the front of the car, dropping to his knees. Greg loomed over him, gun still raised. Harry's pleas filled the air, desperate and raw.

"Please, don't—"

I squeezed my eyes shut. Another shot rang out.

When I opened them, Harry lay motionless, blood seeping into the dirt. I stared at my trembling, bloodstained hands. In that moment, I felt like everything good in me was bleeding out too.

The gunshot's echo faded, leaving an eerie silence. Greg moved with mechanical precision, rifling through Harry's pockets. I stood frozen, unable to process what I'd just witnessed.

"Help me with the body," Greg grunted, trying to drag Harry toward my Thunderbird's trunk.

The reality of the situation crashed over me. "I've been shot, Greg!" I screamed, my voice high and unfamiliar. My hands clutched at my dress, feeling the warm wetness seep through the fabric.

"Use the blanket from the back to stop the bleeding," he said, his voice devoid of emotion. "Then you're driving. But first, help me with the body."

"I can't!" The words caught in my throat as bile rose. The thought of touching Harry's lifeless form threatened to shatter what was left of my sanity.

Greg lost it. He spun me around, his fingers digging into my arms. "You're gonna try!" he snarled, face inches from mine. "Understand? Now lift!"

We struggled with Harry's weight, unable to hoist him into the trunk. Greg finally gave up, rolling the body into the ditch instead. Then he shoved me toward the driver's side. "Drive!" he barked.

"I don't know where to go..." I sobbed, my chest heaving as I fought for air.

"I'll lead. You follow," Greg ordered, already moving toward Harry's car.

As Greg pulled out in front, the full weight of what we'd done crushed me. I wanted to squeeze my eyes shut, to wake up from this nightmare. Instead, I put the car in gear, following Greg's taillights deeper into the darkness.

CHAPTER 7

Escape

The world blurred around me as I followed Greg's orders, moving mechanically.

"I need to make a call," Greg said, his voice cutting through the fog in my mind. He parked Harry's car a few miles down the road, then directed me to the passenger seat of my Thunderbird.

At a pay phone, Greg stepped out. I sat motionless, staring at nothing, my mind replaying the gunshot on an endless loop.

Greg returned, muttering, "Can't reach him."

"Who?" The question slipped out before I could stop it.

"I'll try again later," he said, dismissing my query. I didn't have the strength to press further.

We drove home, each bump in the road sending a jolt of pain through my side, where the bullet had grazed me. By the time we arrived, it was late. The porch light illuminated a familiar face through the window: my brother Jeff, who was watching my son. My sister Jennifer was there, too, but she was asleep in another room.

Greg rushed us toward the door, but Jeff's eyes narrowed as he noticed my limp.

"What's going on? What's wrong with Judy?" Jeff demanded, stepping forward.

"She's not feeling well," Greg said smoothly, steering me past. We hurried to my bedroom, the lock clicking behind us with finality.

"Change your clothes," Greg ordered, tossing me a trash bag. My fingers felt clumsy as I peeled off the bloodstained dress, stuffing it into the bag with trembling hands.

At the sink, I scrubbed at my hands, watching red-tinged water swirl down the drain. The face in the bathroom mirror looked hollow, unrecognizable. I realized with surprise that I was looking at myself.

We returned to the car after I'd changed, and its interior felt suffocating as we drove through the night.

Greg's voice cut through the silence, "Your clothes, your shoes—they're too risky. We need to destroy everything. Leave nothing for the cops."

We wound through bumpy country roads in the pre-dawn darkness. Greg's eyes darted back and forth, searching. Suddenly, he jerked the wheel, pulling off near a ditch.

"This is it," he muttered, killing the engine. The silence that followed was deafening.

Without a word, Greg stepped out, disappearing into the

field. I watched through the windshield as he reappeared, my bloodstained clothes in his hands. The smell of liquor wafted through the open car door as he doused the fabric.

A match flared in the darkness. Flames leapt up, devouring my dress and shoes. I watched, transfixed, as the evidence of our crime turned to ash.

We drove on, stopping at another deserted lot. This time, Greg ordered me to stay in the car. In the dim light, I could see him digging frantically with his bare hands. He pulled out a box—a portion of Harry's jewelry, I realized with a jolt—and the gun. Both disappeared into the freshly dug hole.

"Let's go," he said, climbing back in, dirt caked under his fingernails. "We've got more to do."

The wound on my side throbbed, a constant reminder of the night's horror. Blood seeped through my makeshift bandage, staining my fresh clothes.

"We can't go to a hospital," Greg muttered, his eyes darting nervously. "Too many questions."

Minutes later, we pulled up to a nondescript house in a quiet neighborhood. Greg disappeared inside, leaving me alone with my thoughts. When he returned, he gestured for me to follow.

Inside, a man—Don Littlejon, an associate of Greg's—eyed the bloodstain on my shirt. "I know a doctor in St. Louis," he said, his voice low. "He'll patch her up, no questions asked."

I swayed on my feet, their words washing over me. How

had this become my reality—shot, burning evidence, meeting criminals in the dead of night?

"We'll take her there," Greg agreed, his voice sounding distant.

The drive to St. Louis passed in a haze of pain and disbelief. But instead of seeking medical help, Greg had other plans.

"We need to meet a fence," he announced. "Sell some of Harry's jewelry."

We ended up at a bank, of all places. Greg disappeared into the vault with the fence, leaving me in the car, pressing against my wound and fighting waves of nausea.

The promise of seeing a doctor faded like a mirage. Greg's priorities were clear—cash and covering our tracks. My well-being became an afterthought.

The St. Louis hotel room felt like a cage. Suddenly, the door burst open. A man with cold eyes and a voice like steel entered. His name was Gary Lacey, and he worked for Don Littlejon.

"Let's get straight to it," he growled. "Don Littlejon sent me here to kill you both."

He sat down, pulling out a gun with a silencer. My eyes darted to the window.

"Don't bother, Judy," he said, following my gaze. "I've got someone by your car. You're not going anywhere."

He laid out our fate with chilling precision. "First, I'll kill Greg. Then Judy, you'll call Don and tell him where those stolen jewels are hidden. I'll take you to a phone for your final call. Lie, and you're dead."

My heart hammered against my ribs. But then, something in Gary's face changed. He stared at me, his brow furrowing.

"You're...you're Tessie's daughter," he said, his voice losing its edge.

I nodded, too shocked to speak.

"I've seen your picture in your mama's shop," he continued, his tone softening.

He took a deep breath and began to speak. His family had been homeless when they came to Missouri. My mother had helped them—clothes, blankets, food. That was Mother all over—always taking care of strays.

"Your mother did right by us," he said, his voice thick with emotion. "I'm not gonna kill you today. Your mother just saved your life."

"What?" I whispered, barely able to comprehend his words.

"Your mother," he repeated. "What she did for my family...that means something."

As the reality of what had just happened sank in, my legs nearly gave out. In that moment, I realized that sometimes, it's not grand gestures that save us. It's the little kindnesses we hardly think about. Mother's simple decency had reached across years to become my guardian angel.

The sheer improbability of it all left me dizzy. In the span of a few minutes, I had gone from facing certain death to being granted life—all because of a few blankets and a warm meal years ago.

Greg's voice took on a desperate edge as he pleaded with Gary. "If you kill me, Don will just have you killed next!" He mentioned Carol White, another victim they'd disposed of for Don. "You'll just be the next in line."

Gary's face turned pale, and Greg seized the moment, proposing a new plan: eliminate Don first, then split the jewelry proceeds.

Something inside me snapped. "You can't keep killing!" I cried, my voice cracking. "This has to end!"

Greg's eyes turned cold. "It's either him or us now. We're loose ends."

"There must be another way!" I begged.

Greg revealed his shocking solution. "The only escape is to disappear. We leave Missouri tonight." He outlined a plan to hide in Alaska with a criminal associate of his.

As he discussed his underworld connections, my stomach churned, and my mind reeled. Criminal contacts? Safehouses? This wasn't the Greg I thought I knew—the charismatic real estate agent, the minister. How long had this been going on? How had I been so blind?

As Greg continued outlining his escape plan, I faced my grim choice: Run or die. Or worse, put my children or family in danger. Abandoning my children was unthinkable, but I saw no alternative.

I wanted to go to the authorities, but I feared Greg's criminal associates would find me or go after my family. His underworld suddenly seemed vast and inescapable. I'd witnessed too much of their ruthlessness now to believe we'd be safe if I stayed in Missouri.

I slumped on the bed, visions of my children flashing before me. It was Angel's birthday—we always celebrated with her favorite cake. And Chip, only four—would he even remember me? I wiped away tears and took a deep breath. Fleeing, as impossible as it seemed, appeared to be my only chance at survival and at protecting my loved ones.

"All right," I said. "I'll go. But I need to say goodbye to my parents first."

Greg nodded, his eyes narrowed with suspicion. With trembling hands, I dialed my mother's number.

"Mother?" My voice quavered. "Can you meet us at the truck stop in Marshfield? In three hours?" I chose a public place deliberately, hoping to shield my family from whatever Greg might do.

After I hung up, Greg's voice turned hard. "You won't be alone with your parents. They'll join us in the car, and you'll tell them we're taking a trip together. Nothing more. Is that clear?"

His eyes locked into mine, the threat implicit. Greg feared I might reveal everything—the manipulation, the murder, our plans to flee to Alaska.

My heart raced as I spotted my mother's familiar Cadillac pulling into the truck stop. Greg and I waited by my car, the tension palpable.

As my parents approached, I forced a smile. "Hi, Mother. Teddy Bear." My voice sounded strange to my own ears.

We all piled into my car, Greg's presence looming over us like a storm cloud. I made stilted small talk, hyper-aware of every word.

After a few excruciating minutes, I turned to my mother.

"Mother, would you accompany me to the restroom?" I struggled to keep my voice steady.

Greg's eyes flashed with rage, but he remained silent. This wasn't part of his plan, but I saw my chance. I had to make sure my mother knew the truth.

The dingy gas station restroom door had barely closed behind us when I collapsed into my mother's arms, sobs wracking my body.

"Mother," I gasped between tears, "there's been a murder." The words tumbled out—Harry, the gun, the plan to flee to Alaska. My mother's eyes widened in shock, her grip on my wrist tightening.

"I couldn't leave without telling you," I whispered. "I don't want you to think I abandoned you all and my children. Please tell Angel and Chip how much I love them." Tears welled in my mother's eyes as she fumbled for a tissue.

I asked for paper and a pen. With shaking hands, I scribbled a note for my children, pressing it into her palm.

"Make sure they know I love them," I pleaded, my voice breaking.

She nodded, unable to speak. We embraced fiercely, then composed ourselves, returning silently to the car.

Greg's suspicious gaze met us, but in that moment, I felt a glimmer of strength. Whatever happened next, someone else knew the truth.

As my parents' car disappeared, Greg erupted. "Why did you go to the bathroom with your mother? I told you to stay in the car!" he hissed as we drove away.

I swallowed hard. "I had to speak with her, to write a note to my children," I said softly. "Telling them how much I loved them and saying goodbye."

Greg's eyes narrowed. "Did you tell her about the murder?"

"No," I lied, my heart pounding. The truth burned in my throat, but I forced it down. If Greg knew I'd confessed, my parents' lives could be in danger. So I kept silent, praying he wouldn't press for details.

After a tense silence, Greg spoke again. "We need someone to know what happened, in case Don Littlejon comes after us. Someone who can't legally talk."

"A lawyer," I said, an idea forming. "Jimmy McMullin in Kansas City. He handled my divorce. He's represented... certain people before."

Greg nodded, a hint of approval in his eyes.

Hours later, we sat in Jimmy's dimly lit office. "Something has occurred," I began, my voice barely above a whisper. "We need to confide in you."

Jimmy held up a hand. "Not a word until you're officially my clients."

After signing the necessary papers, Greg asked me to wait outside. I sank onto a leather couch in the reception area, my side throbbing with each breath.

An eternity seemed to pass before Greg emerged, his face unreadable. "It's done," he said, handing Jimmy a slip of paper. "This is how to reach us in Alaska."

As we left for the airport, I caught a glimpse of my reflection in the office window. The woman staring back at me was a stranger—pale, haunted, stepping into a future I couldn't begin to imagine.

"We've made it," Greg said as the plane touched down, his hand squeezing mine. I forced a smile, his touch sending a shiver down my spine. The familiar skyline of home felt like a distant memory now.

Two figures approached us at the airport. "Loretta and Lee," Greg introduced them. As we drove to our new "home," I learned that Loretta was Lee's girlfriend—and Greg's ex.

Our new apartment felt more like a prison than a home. I would help Loretta with chores and meals. Often, I'd catch her watching me, her eyes filled with a mixture of curiosity and something else I couldn't quite place.

At night, lying next to Greg, my mind would race. The image of Harry's lifeless body haunted me. The ache of separation from my children felt like a physical wound. And always, there was the fear—would Greg decide I was too much of a liability?

Greg had confiscated my ID, my personal records, even my phone. "It's for our safety," he'd say, but his eyes told a different story. Cut off from the world, from my family, I felt like a ghost.

In the dark of night, I'd entertain wild fantasies of ending Greg's life as he slept. But fear always held me back. What if I failed? What would happen to my children then?

So I existed, day by day, a shadow of my former self. Each morning, I'd wake up wondering: Is today the day Greg decides I'm no longer useful? Is today the day it all ends?

Alaska's endless nights seemed to mirror Greg's descent into darkness. His new venture—dealing cocaine and quaaludes by the truckload—turned our apartment into a revolving door of shady characters.

Greg's moods swung wildly, his eyes alternating between manic energy and cold detachment. One particularly bleak day, Greg announced we were going to a mountain resort. "To shake things up," he said.

Once we got to the resort, Greg disappeared into the crowd, leaving me alone at the bar. The whiskey burned my throat, a poor substitute for the warmth of home.

Then I saw him—Greg, leaning close to two women, his hand on one's waist. Something inside me snapped. I told Greg I was going back to our room. The elevator ride was a blur of anger and despair.

In our room, I tore through Greg's suitcase like a woman possessed. Pill bottles rattled as I pried them open, swallowing handful after handful. If I was going to die, it'd be on my terms, not his.

The door burst open. Greg's eyes widened in shock, then narrowed in fury. "You stupid b*tch!" he roared. "What are you doing? You'll get us caught!"

His hands reached for me, but it was too late. The world tilted, then faded to black.

What followed was a series of disjointed images: the whir of helicopter blades, frantic voices, the jolt of a defibrillator. I learned later that the paramedics had to land in a small town to revive me before flying on to Anchorage.

When I finally surfaced from the darkness, Greg's face

swam into view. His expression was a mask of fury, but his voice was chillingly calm. "Don't you dare breathe a word of what we did, or you'll regret it," he threatened.

My body felt leaden, my mind foggy. Before I could fully process his words, Greg was checking me out of the hospital, his grip on my arm bruisingly tight as he steered me to his waiting car.

My suicide attempt had ripped control from Greg's hands, and he couldn't bear it. Back at the apartment, his fury exploded. His fingers dug into my throat, pressing, squeezing. I gasped for air as dark spots danced in my vision. Then, suddenly, he flung me aside like a discarded toy.

For days, Greg's eyes followed my every move, a predator watching its prey. He returned one afternoon, a bag from a clothing store in hand. "Put these on," he ordered, tossing me a pile of turtlenecks. The soft fabric felt like a noose against the tender bruises on my neck.

"You're not leaving the apartment," he added.

The days crawled by, tension building like a pressure cooker about to blow. One night, hushed voices pulled me from a fitful sleep. I crept to the door, easing it open a crack.

Loretta's voice, tight with anger, drifted through. "They can't stay here, Lee. It's too dangerous."

"We promised Greg—" Lee began, but Loretta cut him off.

"I don't care what we promised. I'm thinking about calling the cops."

My heart thundered in my chest. Greg had sworn Lee

would keep us hidden, no questions asked. Now we were trapped with people itching to turn us in.

For a moment, I considered confronting Loretta to plead our case. But fear held me back. If I connected with her, even for a moment, would they kill me? Would Greg see it as a betrayal? Would Loretta and Lee end up as two more bodies he needed to dispose of?

I retreated to my bed, still weak from my overdose. As I lay there, I realized with chilling clarity: One wrong move, one wrong word, and I might be next on Greg's list.

About two weeks after the overdose incident, Greg moved us to a different apartment in the same complex, leaving Loretta and Lee behind.

One crisp morning, the shrill ring of the phone shattered our uneasy peace. Greg's face drained of color as he listened then hung up. "We've got to go. Now," he said, his voice tight. "Jimmy McMullin says we're being watched. Start packing."

We threw our belongings into suitcases. Greg was in the middle of a drug deal, so we couldn't fly out immediately. Instead, we sought refuge at another associate's place, the hours crawling by as we waited for the buyer to show with the money.

Suddenly, the wail of sirens pierced the air. Blue and red lights flooded the windows, casting eerie shadows across the room.

"Come out with your hands up!" an officer's voice boomed through a bullhorn.

Greg's eyes darted wildly. He snatched up his gun. "I'm checking the garage," he said. "You hide in the closet."

I obeyed, my heart pounding so loudly I was sure they could hear it outside. Minutes felt like hours in that dark, cramped space.

Then, a deafening crash. Footsteps thundered through the house. The closet door flew open. Rough hands yanked me out, twisting my arms behind my back. The cold bite of handcuffs against my wrists almost felt like relief.

As they read me my rights, I caught a glimpse of Greg being led out in cuffs. Our eyes met for a brief moment. In that instant I knew: The running was over.

Outside, surrounded by flashing police cars, I kept my gaze fixed on the ground. A twisted sort of hope bloomed in my chest. We were going back to Missouri, back to my family, back to a chance at truth and justice. No more hiding, no more drugs. Now, I could finally tell the authorities everything—about Greg's schemes, about Harry Klein's murder.

They arrested us on December 20, 1981. As the year drew to a close, we boarded a plane back to Missouri, landing on New Year's Eve. It felt fitting somehow—the end of one chapter, the uncertain beginning of another.

CHAPTER 8

The Trial

The jail cell felt like another world, one I was wholly unprepared to navigate. My family visited often, their faces etched with concern, but they were as lost as I was when it came to the complexities of a criminal trial.

Greg slithered his way back into this void of uncertainty. It might seem unbelievable that I could trust the man who'd dragged me into murder, torn me from my family, and left bruises on my neck. The very reason I was behind bars.

But here's the thing about abuse: It rewires your brain. I'd spent most of my life in this twisted dance, forgiving men who hurt me, convinced that their moments of kindness outweighed the pain they caused. This kind of thinking is not unlike Stockholm syndrome, where hostages begin to sympathize with their captors. Why? It's a survival tactic when hope seems lost.

Greg knew this dance better than anyone. His words, dripping with honey, found their way through the cracks in my defenses.

"Don't worry about a thing, Judy," he'd write in long, flowery letters. "If we can get through this, we can get through anything."

"You've always been my soulmate," he'd gush, as if he'd never raised a hand against me.

He painted pictures of our future after this "misunderstanding" was cleared up. We'd be tried separately, but he swore we'd weather it together. "They'll never find you guilty," he promised.

I knew, somewhere deep down, that I was ignoring the obvious: He'd killed a man and used me to do it. But in my shattered state, anything familiar felt safe, even if that familiarity was laced with danger. So I let him take charge of our defense, buying into his dreams and lies hook, line, and sinker. It was easier than facing the terrifying unknown alone.

As I waited for the legal system to hear my case, months stretched into almost a year. I ached for Angel's infectious laugh and Chip's sleepy goodnight kisses, but I couldn't bear the thought of them visiting me here. How could I explain the bars, the guards, the harsh reality of prison to my children?

At night, I'd lie awake, imagining their soft breathing in the next room. My arms felt empty without them to hold. During the day, I'd catch myself reaching for a hand that wasn't there, my heart clenching at the absence.

My siblings' confused faces haunted me. I'd always been their rock, the one they turned to in hard times. Now, I was the source of their pain and bewilderment. The irony wasn't lost on me as I sat in my cell, powerless to comfort them.

When my family visited, I'd plaster on a smile, my voice steady as I spoke of hope and better days. "It'll all work out," I'd say, even as despair clawed at my insides. Their worried eyes saw through my façade, but I couldn't bear the thought of them losing sleep over me.

"Mother, please stay away from the trial," I begged during one visit. The image of Greg or his associates targeting her made my blood run cold. "We'll have good memories again someday," I promised, hoping I wasn't lying.

There were moments when the weight of it all felt crushing. The cold metal of my bunk would beckon, whispering of an easy way out. But then I'd think of my family—of Angel and Chip growing up without a mother—and I'd find a reservoir of strength I didn't know I possessed.

It wasn't pretty or heroic. Most days, it was just putting one foot in front of the other, breathing in and out. But sometimes, that's all you've got. And for my family, it had to be enough.

In the stark confines of my cell, I found myself reaching for the Bible my mother had brought. My history with the church had been complicated, but there I sat, thin pages rustling beneath my fingers, searching for answers I wasn't sure existed.

I had no method, just desperation. I'd flip to random pages, wrestling with the archaic language of King James. It was the only version I knew, a relic from my childhood church.

As days blurred by, something stirred within me. Maybe it was my mother's unwavering faith finally taking root, or perhaps in this stripped-down existence, those ancient words found fertile ground.

This wasn't a grand spiritual awakening. I was a drowning woman grabbing the only life preserver in reach. I couldn't pick up inner peace at the jail canteen, and my family was already buckling under the weight of my mess.

So I prayed, not just mouthing words from childhood, but pouring out my heart. I begged for wisdom, strength, and courage. I pleaded for my children's safety, imagining them adrift without me.

But there were nights when fury consumed me. I'd grip the Bible tight, knuckles white, demanding answers. "Why?" I'd whisper fiercely. "Why let this happen? You could end this nightmare with a thought."

I found solace in Job's story. Here was a man who dared question God. So I followed suit, figuring if God gave us these emotions, He could handle some raw truth.

When I finally let loose, it wasn't pretty or reverent. But in that unfiltered honesty, I found an unexpected peace. Like maybe God could absorb my anger and still keep me close.

In my darkest moments, I wondered if this was some brutal test. Was God showing me how precious my kids were by ripping us apart? The thought left me gasping, reeling.

But even as I raged, a stubborn spark of hope refused to die. Maybe, just maybe, God would wring something good from this mess. So I kept reading, kept praying, even when it felt like shouting into a void.

They tried me before Greg—the alleged accomplice before the actual shooter. The courtroom descended into farce from the start, as prosecutors built their case against me with bricks of flimsy evidence.

The prosecution flew Loretta in from Alaska to testify. I learned that she'd turned us in and gotten a reward from the state. In the courtroom, her words spun a web of lies so intricate, I almost lost myself in its complexity. "She confessed everything to me," Loretta declared, her voice steady. I could see it in her eyes—she still loved Greg and would say anything to save him.

The parade of false witnesses continued. A jewelry store clerk swore I'd called asking for Harry Klein. Greg was connected to Don Littlejon, who'd struck an immunity deal and gift-wrapped Greg's version of events for the prosecution.

And then there was my Thunderbird—my silver symbol of freedom turned weapon against me. Those MI TURN plates, once a declaration of independence, now became a beacon for witnesses. Someone claimed they'd seen it on that lonely country road the night of the murder.

I watched as the prosecutors wove these threads together—my car at Cody's Bar, then near the crime scene. In their lies, my beloved Thunderbird might as well have been a getaway car.

Sitting there, drowning in this sea of deception, I felt the cruel irony. The very things that had represented my newfound freedom—my car, my independence—were now the tools of my undoing.

My defense felt like a paper boat in a hurricane. My few character witnesses—my friend Nolene, some girls from my salon—took the stand, but their well-meaning words were barely audible over the thunderstorm of the prosecution. Even their innocent mention of Harry calling the salon became another nail in my coffin.

"We should get Gary Lacey on the stand," I whispered urgently to my lawyer. "He knows the truth."

My attorney shook his head. "He's threatening to plead the fifth. It won't help us."

With each passing day, my frustration mounted. This lawyer had gotten actual mafia killers off the hook, yet he seemed to be rolling over without a fight.

"Let me testify," I pleaded one afternoon, desperation clawing at my throat. "I can show them my scar, tell them what really happened."

Again, he shut me down. "Cross-examination would destroy you," he muttered, not meeting my eyes.

So I sat, a silent volcano of fury, as lie after lie piled up around me. I forced a smile for my family, especially my mother, who faithfully attended each day. But that façade became my undoing: "The happy killer," the media dubbed me, their pens dripping with sensationalism.

It felt like salt in an open wound. My parents were furious, especially when a local store started advertising an issue of the salacious *Inside Detective* magazine that included my story. "Get the true story of Judy Henderson here! Diamonds aren't always a girl's best friend!" the store's sign read.

My mother, bless her heart, wasn't having any of it. She marched right over, tore down that sign, and read the store owner the riot act. My mother recounted the story to me on one of her jail visits, her eyes ablaze with anger. When I saw the fierce protectiveness in her face, I felt a flicker of warmth. No matter the outcome, I realized, I'd always have someone in my corner.

CHAPTER 9

Verdict

The truth crept up on me in that jail cell, each realization more nauseating than the last. Greg's plan hadn't started with Harry Klein's murder—it had begun the moment Gina mentioned Harry in that Kansas City bar.

I could see it now, clear as day: Every sweet word, every tender moment had been another thread in his web. While I clung to faith in the system and his loyalty, Greg was orchestrating my downfall from the shadows.

One afternoon, the jail matron let something slip. "Your boyfriend's been meeting with other lawyers," she said. "Not just that McMullin fellow."

My stomach dropped. I cornered Jimmy during his next visit, peppering him with questions. His answers were a maze of legal jargon, each word sliding away like water on glass.

"Jimmy," I finally said. "We need to make a deal with the prosecutor. I'll tell them everything about Greg if they go easy on me."

He nodded, promising to return with news. A little later that day, he came back shaking his head. "They won't budge," he said, not quite meeting my eyes. "They've got other witnesses."

It wasn't until much later that I learned the bitter truth: Jimmy never even asked for a deal. Somewhere along the line, Greg had gotten to him, and I'd been left in the dark.

As the trial date loomed closer, dread settled over me like a heavy fog. I'd thought sharing an attorney with Greg might lead to the truth. Instead, I'd handed him the rope to hang me with.

The night before the verdict, my fingers trembled as I folded clothes into cardboard boxes. Nearly seven months had crawled by since the arrest, each day a battle against the crushing weight of uncertainty. But tonight, on the eve of judgment, I allowed a fragile hope to bloom.

It was the early eighties, and Missouri jails still permitted a slice of the outside world within their walls. My family had brought clothes that smelled of home, toiletries that weren't state-issued—small anchors to the life I'd left behind. I ran my hand over a soft sweater, imagining the freedom it represented.

Closing my eyes, I let myself dream of Angel and Chip. I could almost taste a home-cooked meal, feel the comfort of my own bed. The fantasy expanded: night air on my skin as I walked under a canopy of stars, answering to no one but myself.

Sleep danced just out of reach that night. The clock on

the wall ticked relentlessly. When the guards finally came to take me to the courtroom, I cast one last glance at my cell, those boxes standing guard. "Today is the day my family comes to take me home," I whispered silently to myself.

The walk to the courtroom felt surreal. Hope fluttered in my chest, a delicate bird ready to take flight. This was just a formality, wasn't it? The truth would emerge, justice would prevail, and I'd walk out of here a free woman.

As I took my seat, I clung to this belief with the desperate conviction of someone who'd forgotten how cruel the world could be. The judge entered and I held my breath, poised on the knife edge between freedom and fate.

July 27, 1982

In the courtroom I fixed my gaze straight ahead, feeling the weight of countless stares on my back. My mind raced through the facts like a mantra: No criminal record. Greg's manipulation. My cooperation. My bullet wound. Justice had to prevail. It just had to.

After both sides' closing arguments were complete, the judge said, "Will the defendant please rise?"

The judge's voice jolted me. My legs felt like jelly as I stood. This was the moment that would cleave my life in two.

The jury foreman's hands seemed to move in slow motion as he unfolded the verdict slip. I gripped the edge of the table, my knuckles white.

"Guilty."

For a heartbeat, the word hung in the air. Then chaos

erupted, confirming the impossible: I'd been condemned as Harry Klein's killer.

My mother's wail sliced through the din, a sound of pure anguish. I wanted to run to her, to shield her from this pain. Instead, I mustered a weak smile, a pitiful attempt at reassurance.

The judge's voice droned on about sentencing options—death or life without the possibility of parole for fifty years. The words barely penetrated the roaring in my ears. How had it come to this?

The world tilted as they led me away. Flashbulbs exploded in the hallway, reporters shouting questions I couldn't comprehend. I moved mechanically, as if watching someone else's nightmare unfold.

Back in my cell, I crumpled in the corner, sobs tearing from my throat. This wasn't fear—it was my mind rebelling against a truth too awful to accept.

Years later, the lead prosecutor in my case, Tom Mountjoy, became an unlikely ally in my fight for freedom. It sounds improbable, but we even struck up a friendship.

My family and friends had long suspected that the aggressive prosecution of my case served a political purpose. The timing was telling—it was a high-profile trial that came just as Tom was positioning himself for election as chief prosecutor. A tough-on-crime image could make or break a prosecutor's career in those days, and a conviction in my case would have burnished that reputation.

Whatever the original motivations, time has a way of

changing perspectives. Over the years, Tom became one of my strongest advocates, quietly supporting my fight for freedom. He showed remarkable courage in reconsidering my case and eventually speaking out for my release. The man who once stood against me in court became one of my most dedicated allies—and remains a friend to this day.

As the courtroom chaos subsided, one detail pierced through my fog of despair: The judge had called me a "relatively minor participant" in the crime.

I clung to that phrase. The verdict condemned me, but the judge had seen the truth. Surely that had to count for something?

Thirty minutes later, shackles biting into my ankles, I was shuffled back into the courtroom for sentencing. Would it be the death penalty, or life without the possibility of parole for fifty years? In other words, was this my final walk as a free woman—or my final walk, period?

The harsh fluorescent lights made me blink as I entered. My parents sat in the gallery, their faces etched with worry lines. I looked away quickly, their pain too raw to bear.

The jurors' eyes skittered past me, finding sudden interest in the floor, the walls, anywhere but my face. I felt myself trembling inside, but years of hiding storms behind a calm face served me well.

"Will the defendant please rise?"

I stood, my heart thundering in my chest. The jury foreman cleared his throat, the sound deafening in the silent room.

"For the charge of capital murder, the jury sentences the defendant to life imprisonment without possibility of parole for fifty years."

Relief washed over me for a split second—I wouldn't die. But that feeling quickly drowned in a tidal wave of despair. I would live, but not truly. Not in a way that mattered.

At thirty-two, my life had been reduced to a number on a jumpsuit. Fifty years stretched before me, an eternity of missed moments and lost possibilities.

The walk back to the cell felt like wading through molasses. Each clank of my shackles echoed in the empty hallway.

Once alone, the dam finally broke. I collapsed onto the thin cot, tears flowing hot and fast. I cried for Angel and Chip, for the birthdays and graduations I'd miss. I cried for my parents and siblings, their anguished faces burned into my memory. I cried for myself, for the life that had just slipped through my fingers.

PART II

CHAPTER 10

New Fish

Before being locked up in the county jail, I'd never seen the inside of a cell. Prison had always been an abstract concept, something that happened to other people, a distant reality I'd only glimpsed through flickering TV screens. In my mind, it loomed as a place of constant vigilance, where only the toughest survived.

As the day of my transfer approached, my stomach churned with dread. I wasn't some hardened criminal— just a woman caught in the undertow of someone else's crime. How could I possibly navigate a world designed for society's outcasts?

The morning of my transfer arrived. As the guard methodically chained my hands and feet, I felt the last wisps of my old life evaporating. The prison van's engine rumbled to life, its vibrations traveling through the metal floor and into my bones. Outside the barred windows, familiar landscapes blurred into a silent farewell.

Dusk was settling as Renz Farm came into view, its

harsh floodlights cutting through the gloom. My breath caught in my throat as we passed through the gates, the ominous clang echoing in the growing darkness.

The van lurched to a stop. I stumbled out, my legs weak from the journey and fear. Before me stood my new home—a behemoth of concrete and steel. Rows of tiny windows stared down, unblinking and uncaring. There would be no hiding here, no escape from this grim reality.

The prison's intake process made the county jail searches seem like a polite pat-down. They herded us newcomers into a stark room, barking orders to strip. We peeled off our clothes, each layer taking with it a shred of dignity. I kept my gaze fixed on the floor, acutely aware of my exposed skin.

"Open your mouth!" "Shake out your hair!" "Lift your foot!" The commands came rapid-fire, reducing us to obedient livestock. I squatted, coughed, and bent over, as I was ordered to spread my butt cheeks for inspection. I felt less human with each passing moment. The lice treatment seared my scalp, its acrid smell making my eyes water. They thrust a blue jumpsuit into my arms—the uniform of a "new fish" in this vast, unfamiliar ocean.

Finally, they led me to a dingy basement cell. As the door clanged shut, the weight of my new reality came crashing down. I curled up on the lumpy cot, my sobs echoing off the bare walls. Any pretense of bravery I'd maintained crumbled like sand.

Tomorrow, I knew, I'd have to piece myself back together

and face this new world. But for now, in the quiet darkness, I allowed myself to break. It was the last time I'd have that luxury for a long, long while.

Those first days, they kept us new fish in a dank basement block, isolated from the main prison. Our only glimpse of the wider world came at mealtimes, when guards herded us upstairs like reluctant cattle.

The cafeteria was a gauntlet of jeers and crude remarks. "Fresh meat!" they'd call, eyes gleaming with predatory interest. "You'll be mine soon..." We huddled together, instinct driving us to seek safety in numbers. These lifers, long removed from society's norms, saw us as rare sport in their monotonous world.

I forced myself to eat, and I tried to appear unfazed. But my insides quivered like jelly. Whispered threats of our "initiation" into general population—GenPop, they called it—followed us back to our cells. Those words echoed in my head as I lay sleepless on my thin mattress, wondering what fresh hell tomorrow would bring.

After a month, they thrust me into GenPop with-out ceremony. The relative safety of the basement van-ished, replaced by a vast room of cubicles where seasoned inmates lived in unsettling proximity. The shared bath-room stripped away any last illusion of privacy, our most basic functions on display under harsh fluorescent bulbs.

Renz Farm, a co-ed facility with about one hundred women, allowed us to wear our own clothes—the state's twisted idea of economy. My new home was a cold, open space with four rows of cubicles that offered more illusion than reality of personal space. A hard cot and a small locker for my meager possessions were my only furnishings. Short walls left us exposed, while large pillars created shadowy corners where anything could happen unseen.

As darkness fell that first night, the crowded dorm amplified every sound into a symphony: the sniffling of addicts, muffled sobs of the despairing, and occasional moans of illicit pleasure.

In the basement, I'd felt a semblance of safety, like a child hiding under covers. But here, I was exposed, an easy target. This wasn't just a bad dream I could wake up from. This was my new life.

In prison, dignity was a luxury we couldn't afford. But the urine drop stripped away whatever scraps of self-respect we had left clinging to our souls.

The order could come at any hour, jolting us from sleep or interrupting precious moments of distraction. "Henderson, give me a drop," a guard would demand, thrusting a wide-mouthed cup at me. Their eyes were flat with boredom, as if this was just another tedious task in their day.

My stomach would instantly knot. Two glasses of water, a plastic cup, and a merciless clock ticking away two hours. Produce, or face solitary confinement—also known as "the hole."

I'd shuffle to the grimy bathroom. The tiles were cold beneath my bare feet as I squatted, exposed and vulnerable. The guard's presence loomed, an impassive witness to this most private act.

My body often rebelled against the command perfor-mance. I'd sit there, muscles tense, willing my bladder to cooperate. Minutes stretched into eternities. The shame deepened with each failed attempt, as if my body was just another piece of prison machinery malfunctioning on cue.

Failure meant a "dirty urine" violation—not for drugs, but for the simple crime of having a shy bladder. The spec-ter of the hole loomed large, a concrete tomb waiting for those who couldn't perform.

In the free world, using the bathroom is a private, unremarkable act. But in prison, it became a battle of will against your own body and the system that sought to con-trol its every function.

Years later, I still sometimes feel the phantom weight of that plastic cup in my hands. It's an invisible scar, unseen but aching all the same—a reminder of how thoroughly prison could strip away not just freedom, but the most basic human dignities.

The fluorescent glow that lit GenPop flickered out, plung-ing the room into darkness. Only then did I let my brave façade crumble.

Silent tears soaked my thin pillow as memories of my children flooded in—their small, warm hands in mine, their laughter echoing from what felt like another lifetime. I clung to these fragments, desperate for any shred of hope that this nightmare would end.

In this alien landscape, I found myself returning to a

familiar habit: prayer. Each night, curled on my hard bunk, I'd whisper words I'd learned as a child. "Our Father, who art in heaven..."

But as days turned to weeks, I felt a gnawing emptiness that solitary prayers couldn't fill. My spirit, starved for connection, craved something more. That's when I saw the notice for prison church services pinned to the bulletin board.

The first Catholic mass I attended was a sensory shock. The pungent incense hung heavy in the air, so different from the harsh antiseptic smell of the prison. Solemn chants replaced the constant cacophony of cell block life. The rituals were foreign, yet I found myself drawn in by their gravity.

In that makeshift chapel, surrounded by women with hollow eyes and hunched shoulders, I felt a spark of something I'd almost forgotten—hope. The priest's words, though often lost in the poor acoustics, seemed to speak directly to the ache in my chest.

As I knelt on the cold concrete floor, the weight of my circumstances pressed down on me. But for the first time since entering these walls, I felt a flicker of peace. This wasn't the fiery faith of my childhood revivals. Instead, it was something quieter, more resilient—a faith tempered by harsh realities yet refusing to be extinguished.

Week by week, in that unlikely sanctuary, I began to piece together a new understanding of myself. I wasn't just inmate Henderson anymore. I was a seeker, a survivor, a mother holding on to hope. And in those moments of shared worship, I found a different kind of freedom—one that no prison walls could contain.

In this world of hardened criminals, I stuck out like a neon sign. Everything about me screamed *target*—my race, my size, my neat clothes, my styled hair. I tried to fade into the background, keeping my eyes down and my voice low, but it was like trying to hide an elephant in a matchbox.

"Look at the princess," they'd sneer, circling like vultures. "Too good for us, ain't she?"

One night, as I was brushing my teeth, the bathroom plunged into darkness. My heart slammed against my ribs. In prison, unexpected darkness never meant anything good.

Heavy footsteps approached. Two voices cut through the black—Steph and Dale.

"Well, well...look who we got here," Steph growled.

"Back off," Dale snapped. "She's mine tonight."

They argued over me like I was a piece of meat at the market. As they bickered, I inched toward the exit, praying for invisibility. Suddenly, bodies crashed against the sink. The sounds of their fight filled the small space—fists hitting flesh, heads slamming against tile.

Just as I reached the door, the lights blazed back on. I bolted.

That night, the bathroom ambush played on repeat in my mind. I'd never felt so hunted, so helpless. In here, my safety was as fragile as an eggshell. I'd narrowly escaped becoming a prize in Steph and Dale's twisted game. The next day, who knew?

Night after night, I lay awake, my body tense as a coiled spring. Every creak, every whisper became a potential threat. The Judy who'd entered these walls was crumbling.

I stared at my reflection in the scratched metal mirror above the sink. The frightened eyes that looked back at me wouldn't survive in this place. Survival, I realized, demanded a metamorphosis.

I had to become someone new, someone as hard and cold as prison steel. I set about building this new self with desperate intensity, burning away every soft edge and vulnerability. The frightened young mother I'd been had no place here.

I practiced my new persona in whispered conversations with my reflection. Gone were the polite phrases and soft tones. I honed my words into weapons, each one sharp and purposeful. The woman who emerged spoke rarely, but when she did, her voice carried the weight of unspoken threats.

"Judy Ann" became a secret, locked away in the deepest recesses of my mind. To the world, to myself, I was now inmate Henderson—cold, hard, belonging among the worst of them.

Anger became my fuel, my armor against the crushing weight of grief. I pictured Greg's face, letting the rage simmer and build. In the prison gym, I pushed my body to its limits, each rep, each lap forging me into something harder, less breakable.

As weeks turned to months, I felt the transformation solidify. The soft edges burned away, leaving behind someone capable of surviving this harsh new world.

My tough girl act didn't fool everyone. One lifer took a particular interest in me—a woman whose crime made even the most hardened inmates shudder. She'd murdered a pregnant woman and her unborn child. Whispers followed her like shadows; she practiced witchcraft, they said.

One afternoon, I returned to find my cubicle in disarray. My stomach dropped as I noticed a single shoe missing. The truth, when it came, was more chilling than any theft.

"She's cursed you," a wide-eyed inmate hissed. "Took your shoe, your hair, even a tissue with your makeup. Says she'll send you tumbling down the stairs."

Logically, it was absurd. A murderous witch? A curse? But logic held little sway in this twisted world. The line between reality and nightmare blurred easily here, and the witch's Wiccan reputation made the threat seem real.

With trembling fingers, I dialed my mother's number. Her voice, when it came, was steady and sure.

"Judy Ann," she said, "keep your Bible open in your cubicle. Satan fears God's Word. No evil will touch you with that shield."

That night, I placed my battered Bible on the small shelf, its pages spread wide. My heart raced with every creak and whisper, but morning came without incident. Days passed. My stolen items reappeared as mysteriously as they'd vanished. The witch's piercing stare found new targets.

For the next thirty-six years, that open Bible became my constant companion. In cells and dormitories across multiple prisons, its worn pages stood guard. To an outsider, it might have seemed foolish. But in a place where hope was as scarce as freedom, that Bible was my talisman—a shield against the darkness that threatened to consume me.

Being in GenPop came with one small mercy: family visits. My heart raced as I watched my parents cross the narrow road to the visiting building. The hum of vending machines faded into the background as I drank in the sight of their familiar, loving faces.

"Judy Ann," my mother whispered, her voice catching. I fell into their embrace, tears streaming down my cheeks, unable to speak past the lump in my throat.

For hours, we talked, carefully sidestepping the raw wound of my case. Instead, they filled the air with stories of Angel and Chip, of backyard barbecues and school plays I'd missed. Each word was a bittersweet reminder of the world beyond these walls.

"How are you really doing?" my stepdad asked, his eyes searching mine.

I faked a smile. "Everything's fine," I lied, painting a rosy picture to ease their worry. The truth—the fear, the loneliness, the daily struggle—stuck in my throat, unspoken.

As visiting hours drew to a close, I clung to them, trying to memorize the feeling of their embrace.

My walk back to the main building was a slow descent into grim reality. My stomach knotted as I approached the strip search area. A line of women stood, faces blank as they removed their clothes, dignity stripped with the fabric.

"Next," a guard barked. I stepped forward, mechanically

following the degrading routine. As I re-dressed, the warmth of my family's love gave way to the cold prison life.

Yet even as shame burned my cheeks, I knew I'd endure this a thousand times over. Those precious hours of connection, of being Judy Ann instead of inmate Henderson, were worth any price. My family was my anchor, my reason to keep going.

Back in my cubicle, I closed my eyes, replaying every moment of the visit. It was a double-edged sword—the joy of connection followed by the pain of separation—but in this strange new world, it was all I had to hold on to.

CHAPTER 11

Hit

Less than a year had passed since I'd been a happy mother. Now, I was a convicted killer, pacing my cell as rage coursed through my veins at Greg, the man who'd seen my history of abuse as clay to be molded for his schemes.

His name alone set my teeth on edge. For the first time, I saw him clearly: a clever sociopath who'd known exactly which strings to pull. And I'd danced to his tune, ignoring every red flag, too dazzled by his charm and empty promises.

As I grappled with my new reality, news of Greg's trial trickled in. He'd fired Jimmy McMullin and hired new attorneys who reshaped the battlefield with surgical precision. Motion after motion, they chipped away at the prosecution's case. It was a master class in legal strategy—everything Jimmy should have done for me, but didn't.

The irony was bitter on my tongue. Greg, the puppet master, was still pulling strings while I paid the price for a crime I didn't commit. In the long, sleepless nights, as I replayed every moment that led me here, I realized my sentence wasn't just about prison time. It was about facing the hard truth of my own naivete and the steep price of misplaced trust.

Then, clarity struck like lightning: I had to testify in Greg's trial, to lay bare the truth of that terrible night. I cornered a prison lieutenant, demanding to speak with Greg's prosecutor.

Months crawled by before they agreed, citing safety concerns. The palpable fear over other inmates seeing me with law enforcement, or Greg catching wind of it, came from knowing I'd have a target on my back. So they smuggled me out, taking back roads to the county jail, far from Greg's reach.

In a sterile interrogation room, I poured out every detail—the manipulation, the violence, the aftermath. For the first time in months, I felt heard, understood. A dangerous spark of hope ignited in my chest. Maybe, just maybe, I could reclaim my life.

As the prosecutors prepared me to be their star witness, a mix of dread and anticipation churned in my gut. This was my shot at redemption, at setting the record straight. But hope is a double-edged sword in prison. It can lift you up, only to drop you harder when reality comes crashing back.

Still, I held on to that sliver of hope as I rehearsed my testimony. Even if it couldn't undo my conviction, bringing Greg to justice felt like a feast after months of starvation. It was all I had left—the chance to right this wrong, to make sure Greg faced the consequences of his actions.

One morning, I felt eyes drilling into my back in the chow line. I kept my gaze down, but a voice cut through the cafeteria din.

"Hey, Judy, sit here!"

I glanced up to see Brandy, all muscle and tattoos, waving me over. When I hesitated, her tone sharpened. "I wasn't asking. Sit."

Laughter rippled through nearby tables. I sat, stomach knotting.

"Prison got you all stressed out?" Brandy asked, a wry smile on her lips.

"Just adjusting," I mumbled.

Her hand brushed mine. I flinched. "Relax," she chuckled. "Unless you want more..."

I fled, cheeks burning, appetite gone.

Later, Brandy cornered me outside the showers. "Been avoiding me?" she asked, arms crossed.

"Just busy," I muttered, clutching my shower caddy like a shield.

"Too busy for friends who want to help you?" Her tone darkened. "That's not smart, Judy."

As I tried to brush past, her hand clamped on my wrist. "You need my help," she hissed, "or you'll end up dead."

My blood froze. "What are you talking about?"

"Word is, someone paid Pam good money to kill you."

The world tilted. "Who?" I whispered.

Brandy's eyes met mine, hard as flint. "Greg."

Greg's plan to silence me sent ice through my veins. He'd already stolen my freedom and reputation. I refused to let him take my life without a fight.

I approached another "fifty-stipper"—a lifer bound by the cruel stipulation of fifty years without possibility of parole. "Hold bust," I whispered, using our code for keeping lookout. "Pam and I need privacy to...chat." She hesitated, then nodded, taking up her post as I slipped into the restroom.

My heart raced as I called out, "Pam? Got a minute?"

She entered, eyes hard. "Fine. What's up?"

I gestured to the bench, forcing a casual tone. "Have a seat. Just want to ask you something."

Pam sat slowly, shoulders tense. I made small talk, waiting for her guard to drop. The moment her eyes flicked away from my hands, I struck.

My fist connected with her cheekbone, a sickening crunch echoing off the tile walls. Pam sprawled backward, shock etched on her face. I pounced, my shoes slamming into her stomach. She gasped, the air gone from her lungs.

Then I saw it in her hand: a flash of metal—her shank. I grabbed her wrist, slamming it against the washers. The blade clattered to the floor. We grappled wildly, but I held strong. She lunged for the weapon, but I pinned her down, my weight pressing her into the cold concrete.

Shouts pierced the air. Guards burst in, strong arms yanking me off Pam. As they dragged me away, I caught glimpses of wide-eyed inmates. The message was clear: Judy Henderson wasn't an easy target anymore.

In solitary, the adrenaline faded, leaving me shaken but

resolute. The scared, polite Judy was gone. In her place stood a woman willing to fight tooth and nail for survival.

As I sat in the dark cell, a harsh truth settled over me: Sometimes, to survive, you have to become the very thing you fear. It wasn't a lesson I'd wanted, but in this brutal world Greg had thrust me into, it was one I'd never forget.

The first time Charlie's fist split my lip, I was nineteen. Over the years, my body learned to read the signs: tightening eyes meant incoming blows, clenched fists promised pain. *Slap. Punch. Kick.* My body became a living archive of suffering.

In that prison bathroom, these instincts took over. As I threw the first punch, I felt Charlie's cruel lessons guiding my hand. My shin, remembering his boot in my gut, knew exactly where to strike to inflict maximum damage.

Now, curled on the cold concrete of solitary, I stared at my throbbing knuckles. The peaceful mother who'd once tended scraped knees seemed a lifetime away. I could almost hear my own voice, gentle but firm, telling my son, "Use your words, not your hands." When had I strayed so far from those roots?

Shame washed over me in waves. I had vowed not to let prison strip my humanity, yet here I was, more beast than mother. But as much as my conscience ached, I couldn't fully regret my choice. Pam would have killed me. The ruthlessness that took over was called up to save me.

As I walked the prison yard the week after, I noticed the change. Inmates who'd once mocked me now fell silent as

I passed. Their glances skittered away, avoiding direct eye contact. I had shown I wasn't an easy target.

But was respect born of violence really what I wanted? Or did some dark part of me relish their newfound wariness?

At night, lying on my thin mattress, I longed for the version of myself who read bedtime stories and kissed skinned knees. Not this anxious, worn-down woman who saw danger at every turn. I had survived, yes, but at what cost?

In the suffocating silence of solitary confinement, my mind wandered to Pam. We were similar in size, but our lives had taken us down very different paths. I remembered the feel of a whisk in my hand, beating cake batter for my kids' birthdays. For Pam, that same grip was more familiar around a shank.

Yet, as I traced the fresh calluses on my knuckles, I realized we weren't so different. Years of flinching at raised voices, of reading moods in the set of a jaw—these had toughened me, just as life had hardened Pam.

When we clashed in that bathroom, the gap between us vanished. I spoke her language of brutality with a fluency that shocked me. For those frenzied moments, we became mirror images—two women locked in a primal struggle for survival.

Years later, Pam and I passed in the yard. Our eyes met for a fleeting second before sliding away. In that moment, I mourned for us both. For the mother I once was, who measured her strength in hugs given, not punches thrown. And for the person Pam could have been, in a kinder world.

Prison didn't just take our freedom; it slowly chipped away at our humanity. The line between victim and aggressor blurred, leaving us in the shadows, yearning for a light we could barely remember.

The crack of the guard's baton against the bars jolted me awake. "Pack up, Henderson. You're moving again."

My heart raced as I stuffed my belongings into a cloth bag. News of the failed hit had reached the prosecution, and now I was caught in a whirlwind of constant motion.

They called it protective custody, but it felt more like a fever dream. The precautions were exhaustive. One day, I'd be in a county jail cell, the next, whisked away to a hidden safehouse. Guards shadowed my every move, their watchful eyes a constant reminder of the invisible target on my back.

"Keep your head down," one guard muttered as we walked through a bustling jail corridor. "Don't make eye contact."

To the other inmates, I was a ghost—nameless, faceless, my purpose a mystery. If anyone showed a flicker of recognition, I'd vanish before they could blink. There could be no weak links, no cracks for Greg's influence to seep through. I was the key to unlocking his crimes, and the prosecution guarded that key with fierce determination.

At night, in whatever new bed I found myself, I'd lie awake listening to the rhythmic footsteps of the guards outside. Part of me felt grateful for their protection, for the knowledge that an entire system was working to keep me out of Greg's reach.

But the constant vigilance wore on me. Each new face, each unfamiliar room, chipped away at my sense of self. I was safe from Greg but exposed in a different way—stripped of identity, of agency, reduced to a piece on the prosecution's chessboard.

As I traced the outline of yet another strange ceiling, a question nagged at me: Was this what freedom felt like? Or had I simply traded one form of captivity for another?

Greg's failed attempt on my life led him to a different kind of murder—the death of truth.

"Henderson, visitors," the guard barked. In a small room, I found my stepfather and our family minister, their faces ashen.

"I'm sorry, Judy. The prosecution can't put you on the stand," my stepfather said, his voice heavy.

"Why?" I cried. "I'm the only one who knows the truth!"

He shook his head. "Four prisoners claim you confessed to them. It's your word against theirs."

My world tilted. Greg had managed to buy off inmates with promises of money and early parole. Years later, they'd confess to their lies, but by then, it would be too late.

"The jury won't believe you," the minister added softly, "not against four other testimonies."

I was enraged. I'd come so close to redemption, only to have Greg snatch it away with more lies. He had resources, power, the ability to manipulate the system from the outside. I had nothing.

Back in my cell, I collapsed, sobs wracking my body. I'd thought I'd hit rock bottom before, but this...this was a new kind of despair. It wasn't just the loss of freedom or dignity. It was the death of hope itself. I fell into the darkest depression of my life.

Even from behind bars, I could picture Greg's performance. His silver tongue had always been his most dangerous weapon—not a gun or a knife, but words that seduced people under his influence.

In my mind's eye, I saw him standing before the jury, eyes gleaming with that familiar, charismatic glint. "Ladies and gentlemen," he'd say, voice smooth as honey, "I stand before you today, not as the monster the prosecution claims, but as a man led astray."

Greg's lawyers had made a bold move, letting him address the jury directly. I could almost feel the spell I'd once fallen under weaving its way through the courtroom.

He'd lock eyes with each juror, his voice breaking just enough to seem genuine. "I, too, was deceived," he'd say. "Used in a terrible miscarriage of justice."

Where prosecutors painted a greedy conspirator, Greg would sculpt the image of a pious minister, a servant of God manipulated by wickedness. He'd quote scriptures with the fervor of a Sunday sermon, speaking of redemption and second chances.

I could picture sympathy blooming in the jurors' eyes.

Greg would no longer be the man on trial for murder—
he'd become their neighbor, their friend, a reflection of
their own struggles and desires for forgiveness.

As I sat in my cell, miles away from the courtroom, I felt
a chill run down my spine. Greg's voice reshaped reality,
bending anyone who listened to his will. No prison could
contain that power.

I pressed my palms against my eyes, trying to shut out
the image of Greg walking free. In the battle of truth ver-
sus Greg's charisma, truth didn't stand a chance.

CHAPTER 12

Bonds

The day after Greg's acquittal, I sat in my cubicle, staring at the gray concrete wall. Each crack and imperfection blurred as tears welled in my eyes. The last ember of hope had finally flickered out.

There would be no prosecutorial miracle, no dramatic courtroom revelation to set me free. The system I'd once believed in had become a cruel joke.

Days turned into weeks. I went through the motions—eating, working, existing—but not truly living. When I filed for clemency, the paperwork felt more like a ritual than a real chance at freedom. It was like praying for lightning to strike twice in the same spot.

One morning, as I watched the sun rise through the barred window, a realization hit me. The world outside these walls continued to spin, but for me, time had frozen. My children were growing up without me, their lives and my family's lives unfolding in a world I could no longer touch.

I picked up a photo of my kids, their frozen smiles a stark contrast to my current reality. If this was to be my home for the next fifty years, I had to find a way to live, not just exist.

It started every morning, with a small act of defiance. Before the sun rose, I'd drag myself out of bed, and while the rest of the prison slept, I stood in front of a mirror, brush in hand.

For the next forty minutes, that mirror became my canvas. With steady hands, I'd sweep mascara across my lashes, blend eyeshadow on my lids, and dust blush on my cheeks. My prison-pale face transformed, becoming something that wouldn't look out of place on a magazine cover.

This daily beautification ritual was my rebellion against the grayness of prison life. After years of being told by the Pentecostal church that makeup was the devil's war paint, there was something downright delicious about dolling myself up each day.

I'd study fashion magazines like they were holy scripture, learning the latest trends and techniques. For me, looking good wasn't about vanity— Okay, who am I kidding? There was definitely a *smidge* of vanity involved.

But it was more than that. It was about survival, a way to remind myself that beneath the shapeless prison uniform, I was still Judy—a woman with her own style, her own identity.

Of course, my routine didn't exactly endear me to everyone. Whispers followed me down the cell block.

"Think she's trading favors for that fancy mascara?"

"Bet she thinks she's better than us."

But it wasn't an act, and it wasn't about superiority. It was about holding on to the woman I used to be, the one who existed before a prison number became my name.

So every morning, I'd ignore the stares and the whispers, losing myself in the graceful motions of foundation and lipstick. In a world that had taken almost everything from me, this was the one piece of myself I refused to let go.

"Hey, you got a square?"

I blinked at the tattooed woman standing before me, her hand outstretched. "I'm sorry, I don't have any...shapes," I replied, confusion evident in my voice.

The woman's face hardened. "Forget it," she muttered, stalking away.

During my first weeks in prison, I felt like I'd landed on another planet. The other inmates spoke a language that, while technically English, might as well have been Martian.

"The E-squad are coming!" someone hissed one day. I watched in bewilderment as everyone scrambled to look busy. Only when I saw the guards around the corner did I understand.

My polite smiles and blank stares were often misinterpreted as snobbery. In reality, I was simply lost in translation. It didn't help when my mother's care packages arrived.

"What in the world?" I muttered, pulling out a fur-trimmed jacket from the box. Next came lingerie from Frederick's of Hollywood.

"Mother, what am I supposed to do with a fur coat in here?" I asked during our next call, exasperation coloring my voice.

The stark contrast between my fashionable clothes and the worn attire of other inmates only widened the gulf between us. I could feel the resentment simmering.

Desperate to bridge this divide, I turned to the one skill I knew could transcend boundaries: my gifts with hair and makeup. At first, the response to my makeshift salon was tepid. But as word spread, my cubicle became a hub of activity. Women arrived with guarded expressions and left with flowing locks and tentative smiles.

"Girl, you've got magic hands," one inmate exclaimed, admiring her reflection in a scratched mirror.

As I worked, my clients chatted, their words a mix of slang and stories. Slowly, I began to decipher their code.

"So a 'square' is a cigarette?" I asked one day, my hands busy with a complicated braid.

The woman in my chair laughed. "You're learning, princess."

Through these interactions, the walls between us gradually crumbled. Over months, I transitioned from outsider to just another member of our eclectic group. In a place where loss was universal, a simple makeover and a listening ear could work wonders.

"Henderson, you've got to try this," an inmate whispered, her eyes gleaming with mischief. She led me to the common area where a small crowd had gathered around the microwave.

The air was thick with an unexpectedly sweet aroma. I peered over shoulders to see a strange concoction bubbling away inside.

"What is it?" I asked, curiosity piqued.

"Cake," she replied with a wink.

I watched in fascination as she mixed a can of Sprite with crushed cookies from the commissary. The unlikely combination went into the microwave, transforming before our eyes.

After carefully spreading melted candy bars over it like frosting, she sprinkled flavored drink mix on top.

"Here," she said, handing me a piece. "Careful, it's still warm."

I took a tentative bite. The sweetness exploded on my tongue. After months of bland prison food, this sweet, moist mouthful was pure joy. For a moment, eyes closed, I could almost imagine I was at a birthday party back home.

"This is...amazing," I murmured, savoring every crumb.

She beamed with pride. "Prison teaches you to get creative," she said.

As we shared our treats, laughter and chatter filled the air. For a brief time, the gloomy cell block faded away, replaced by something almost...normal.

These small comforts sustained us. A shared recipe, a comforting word, a secret joke—small acts of kindness that sprouted in the harshest soil. On Sundays, hymns from the prison church service would float through the halls, voices raised in hope. Even the darkest humor became a shared language of survival.

"Another day in paradise," we'd quip, finding strength in our ability to laugh at our circumstances. In this place where time stood still, we learned to measure our days not by the calendar, but by moments of growth and small victories—like perfecting the ratio of Sprite to cookies in our makeshift desserts.

The clanging of the visitors' room door set my heart racing. I smoothed my hair, plastered on a smile, and there they were—my children, led in by my friend Nolene.

"Mom!" Angel's voice cracked as she rushed into my arms. Chip hung back, his eyes wide and uncertain.

For the next three hours, we existed in a bubble of forced normalcy. We played board games, shared jokes, and I listened intently to tales of school drama and neighborhood adventures.

"And then Tommy said..." Angel's animated chatter filled the air, while I savored every gesture, every inflection of her voice.

I never mentioned my case or the hardships of prison. They didn't need that burden. Instead, I focused on being the mother they needed—strong, optimistic, present.

But reality always lurked at the edges. After they left, the mask slipped. Alone in my cell, I allowed myself to crumble, the weight of missed moments crushing me.

Visits became rarer as time passed. Charlie forbade Chip from coming after he turned five. The next time I saw him, he was sixteen, driving to the prison by himself.

In between these precious reunions, phone calls kept me connected to the children and to my siblings, especially during holidays. As Thanksgiving or Christmas approached, tension in the prison rose. We'd line up, desperate for our turn at the phones.

"Mother?" My voice would quaver as I heard her familiar hello.

"Oh, Judy Ann," she'd say, and suddenly I was home again, smelling her famous cooking, hearing the bustle of family in the background.

"Tell me everything," I'd plead, and she'd paint a picture of the gathering I couldn't attend—the decorations, the food, the laughter.

But one image stood out above all others: an empty chair at the table, my photograph propped up on the seat. This simple gesture, repeated at every holiday and celebration, became a powerful symbol of my absence and my family's unwavering hope for my return.

I'd close my eyes, picturing that vacant spot at the table. In my mind, I could see the festive decorations, the steaming dishes, laughter and conversation flowing around that silent reminder of my absence. That empty chair was both a wound and a promise—a visual representation of the hole in our family's heart, but also a stubborn declaration that my place would always be saved, waiting for the day I could fill it again.

Hope, fragile but persistent, lifted me to reclaim my place at that table, no longer just a photograph, but flesh and blood, home at last.

When the calls and visits ended and reality set in again, I found myself grappling with something even more elusive than my family's love: my faith. Holding on to belief in prison is like trying to grow flowers in concrete. It takes stubbornness, maybe even a little miracle.

I'd been tending to those stubborn seeds of belief for a while now, occasionally attending Catholic services that were refreshingly different from my Pentecostal upbringing. But doubt was a persistent weed, choking out whatever fragile sprouts of faith managed to push through.

How could I reconcile the God of my childhood—the one who loved sparrows and little children—with the reality of my unjust imprisonment? I'd shuffle into church services, mouthing familiar hymns, offering up a half-hearted prayer when things got rough. But true faith? That was as elusive as freedom itself.

The strict doctrines I'd been raised on now felt suffocating. All those *thou shalts* and *thou shalt nots* that once had seemed like a direct line to Heaven now felt like just another set of prison bars.

Yet, deep inside, a stubborn spark refused to be extinguished. It was a pilot light of faith, flickering but steady. Slowly, painfully, I began to untangle my beliefs from the barbed wire of rigid doctrine. Maybe God was bigger than the box the Pentecostal church had tried to contain Him in. Maybe my relationship with the divine didn't need fire-and-brimstone sermons as a middleman.

It was in this spiritual limbo that I found myself chosen for a program called Residents Encounter Christ. A dozen of us "lifers" were selected as pioneers for this grand experiment in rehabilitation.

Being a lifer in prison was akin to being the eldest sibling in a dysfunctional family—a role I knew intimately well. We were the unofficial peacekeepers, our presence a silent but powerful force in maintaining order. A stern glance or a quietly spoken word from one of us could quell a budding riot or defuse a volatile situation faster than any guard's baton.

Our very existence formed the bedrock of the prison's delicate social structure. For us, these concrete walls and steel bars weren't a temporary stop on the way back to freedom—they were home. This permanence forced us to carve out meaning within these confines.

The prison administration recognized our unique position. They strategically placed lifers on every unit, understanding that our mere presence often kept the peace more effectively than any official measures. We were living reminders of the consequences of unchecked violence or repeated infractions.

When the administration introduced the spiritual program, they chose us lifers deliberately. They understood that if they could reach us—if they could help us find purpose and meaning—the effect would ripple out through the entire prison population. We were the pebbles thrown into the pond, our transformation potentially creating waves that could touch every corner of this enclosed world.

As I entered the chapel that first morning of the Residents Encounter Christ retreat, my skepticism weighed heavily. Years of disappointment had taught me to expect little. But the moment I crossed the threshold, something shifted.

"Welcome." A volunteer greeted me, her smile warm

and genuine. "Would you like a cinnamon roll? They're fresh from the oven."

The aroma of warm bread wafted over to me, a reminder of life beyond these walls.

Over the next few days, the volunteers' kindness began to chip away at my defenses. During a sharing session, I found myself opening up.

"I...I've done things I'm not proud of," I admitted, my voice barely above a whisper.

The volunteer beside me simply nodded. "We all have," she said softly. "But that doesn't define you."

Her words hit me like a physical force. For the first time in years, someone was seeing me—not my crimes, not my prison number, but me.

As the retreat progressed, I witnessed even the toughest lifers breaking down. My tears flowed freely, too, more than I'd shed in the past decade. But these weren't the bitter tears of despair I'd grown accustomed to. They were cleansing, washing away years of accumulated pain.

On the final night, we shared communion. As the bread was passed around, a volunteer turned to me.

"You know," she said, breaking the bread, "in God's eyes, we're all the same. Broken, but loved."

I nodded, the lump in my throat blocking my voice. As I took the bread, I felt a connection I hadn't experienced in years.

When I crawled into my bed that last night, the world didn't seem quite so bleak. For the first time in years, I felt truly seen—not by the system or other inmates, but by something greater. I hadn't been forgotten or abandoned.

I'd just been too wrapped up in my own noise to hear the quiet whisper of grace that had been there all along.

The scent of incense lingered in my hair as I waited for my turn at the prison phone. My fingers traced the outline of the small plastic rosary hidden in my pocket, a souvenir from the Residents Encounter Christ program. The familiar click of the connection barely registered before I blurted out my news.

"Mother, I think I'm going to become Catholic!"

The silence on the other end was deafening. Then, "The Catholics?! Oh no. No, ma'am. Judy Ann, you will not!" Mother's voice crackled with the intensity of a fire-and-brimstone sermon.

I bit back a laugh. Here I was, a middle-aged woman doing hard time, and my mother could still make me feel like a chastised teenager.

As I hung up, I caught my reflection in the scratched metal above the phone. The woman staring back at me looked different somehow—softer around the edges, a spark in her eyes that hadn't been there before.

Later that night, lying on my bunk, I closed my eyes and transported myself back to the retreat. The warmth of acceptance washed over me again, as tangible as a quilt on a cold night. It was a feeling I'd chase in the coming months, especially on the dark days when doubt crept in like a fog.

One particularly rough evening, I found myself in the prison chapel. I knelt, the hard floor a reminder of where I was, but the peace in the air a promise of something more.

"I don't understand all of this," I whispered to the stillness. "But I'm trying."

As the words left my lips, a weight seemed to lift. My faith, once a rigid set of rules, was transforming into something living and breathing—a companion on this journey, rather than a judge.

The next time Mother called, her voice was tentative. "How's that...program going?"

I smiled, recognizing the olive branch. "It's good, Mother. They've opened it up to other denominations now."

Her sigh of relief was audible. "Well, that's...that's nice, Judy Ann."

As we chatted, I realized that my spiritual journey wasn't just changing me—it was creating ripples that touched even those beyond these walls. The God I was discovering was big enough for Catholics, Pentecostals, and even a lifer like me.

No darkness could erase what I'd experienced in those three days. I might not always be able to hear it clearly, but I knew now that God's call was always there, echoing through the emptiness. And at long last, my ears were open, ready to listen.

CHAPTER 13

The Governor

The sharp clack of boots on concrete echoed through the corridor. I tensed, recognizing the sound. An officer rounded the corner, her eyes locking onto me.

Before I could react, she slammed me against the wall, her forearm pressing against my throat. The rough concrete bit into my back as I struggled to breathe.

"If I had my way," she hissed, her face inches from mine, "I'd strip you of that makeup and stuff you in a prison dress."

The pressure on my throat increased for a moment before she released me with a final shove. As she stalked away, I slumped against the wall, gasping and choking out apologies to the empty air.

Later that night, a guard appeared at my cell. "Henderson, Lieutenant Wyrick wants to see you."

My stomach churned as I followed him to the office. Lieutenant Wyrick's face was unreadable as I entered.

"Sit down," he said, his voice gruff. I perched on the edge of the chair, hands clasped tightly in my lap.

"You've got a target on your back, Henderson," he continued. "Some staff think you're acting too good for this place. They want to bring you down." He fixed me with a hard stare. "Best toughen up. The bullying's just starting."

As I left his office, the prison's fluorescent lights seemed harsher, the shadows deeper. Every face I passed suddenly looked like a potential threat. How much of myself would I have to erase to survive here? I wondered. How much Judy would be left when all was said and done?

"Toughen up," I whispered to myself.

The days following Lieutenant Wyrick's warning blurred into a relentless assault. My neatly folded clothes became targets for "random" searches, leaving my cell in disarray. Letters from home mysteriously "vanished," and meal calls were conveniently forgotten.

Guards' sneers echoed through the halls: "She thinks she's too good for this place!"

I never felt that way, but with my manicured nails, styled hair, and hint of lip gloss, I understood how they might see me that way. In a federal prison, which included wealthier inmates serving time for white-collar crimes, I might have blended in. Here, among women from small towns and rural areas, I was an alien.

Things got worse with the guards over the next few weeks, but I didn't back down.

"Henderson!" a guard barked. "Warden wants to see you."

The warden's eyes narrowed as I entered.

"You're causing problems," he said flatly. "Your attitude is disrupting the order here."

I straightened my spine. "Sir, I'm just trying to maintain some dignity—"

"Dignity?" he scoffed. "This isn't a country club, Henderson. You'd do well to remember that."

As I left his office, I made a decision. I wouldn't bend.

The next day, when another officer mocked my appearance, I forced a laugh. "Won't matter soon! I'm going home!"

Her face darkened. "Keep dreaming, princess."

That evening, a friendly chat with Officer Wendy through the dorm gate landed me in solitary, accused of attempted bribery. Ten days later, I emerged, blinking in the harsh light. Wendy wouldn't meet my eyes.

They cycled me in and out of the hole, each stint meant to break me. Random searches, degrading tasks like scrubbing baseboards with a toothbrush—it was all part of their game. But with each slam of that solitary door, my resolve hardened.

"You'll never win!" I'd yell into the emptiness, doing jumping jacks to keep my mind and body active.

My defiance didn't go unnoticed. Inmates started calling me "the Governor," a nickname that only seemed to infuriate the guards more.

One morning, a guard appeared at my cell. "Pack up. You're moving."

She led me down unfamiliar corridors, past cells housing the most violent offenders. We stopped in front of a heavy steel door. Now I saw the true cost of my defiance.

"Welcome to the Incorrigibles wing," she sneered, shoving me inside. "Have fun, Henderson."

The heavy steel door of the Incorrigibles wing clanged shut behind me. Eyes followed my every move as I walked to my assigned bunk, my footsteps echoing in the sudden silence. I felt their gazes like physical touches, probing for weakness. Maybe I'd kept my dignity, but at what price?

Over the next few days, I learned to keep my eyes down but my ears open, to move with purpose even when I felt lost. But one afternoon, I returned to find my locker door hanging open, its meager contents scattered.

I grabbed my padlock, slipped it into a sock, and swung it against my locker with all my might. The metallic clang reverberated through the wing.

"I don't know which b*tch took my sh*t, but I've had enough!" I yelled, pacing back and forth. "Whoever crosses me again, it's on!"

Silence fell, heavy and thick. I could feel the shift in the air, the recalculation happening behind watchful eyes. That night, I sat on my bunk, makeshift weapon in hand, heart pounding. But no one came.

In the days that followed, whispers trailed me like shadows. Women who'd once sneered now gave me a wide berth. My bluff had worked—unpredictability became my new armor.

Over time, the act became real. Constant threats left me quick to anger, reflexes primed for attack. I never sought trouble, but I wouldn't cower either. The old Judy might have; this new one had grown a thick skin.

I'd become someone new, someone capable of violence and fury. But each night, listening to the symphony of snores and nightmare whimpers, I shed my hard exterior. In the darkness, I was still just a woman missing her children, aching for home.

My hand cramped as I scrawled on yet another complaint form. But I kept writing. Inadequate medical care. Abusive staff. Insufficient mental health resources. The list grew longer each day.

"Henderson," a guard called, "your sister's here."

I followed her to the visiting room, my heart lightening at the sight of a familiar face. As we hugged, I caught sight of a cart piled high with care packages from Mother.

"All this has to go back," a guard interrupted, his voice flat. "Inmates can't have any of it."

"But those are my boxes!" I protested. "My mother sent them to me."

"Well, you can't have 'em."

"Yeah, you know why I can't have them?!" I yelled, my voice rising. "Because I won't sleep with the property room officer! That's why!"

My sister's eyes widened in shock, then narrowed in fury. She joined my shouting until they escorted her out, the cart of supplies rolling away with her.

Thirty days in solitary was the price for my outburst. But as I sat in the dark, cramped cell, I knew I'd hit a nerve. Fred's name had been whispered among inmates for months—the property officer who demanded sexual favors in exchange for basic necessities.

My family's support fueled my resolve. Phone calls to

representatives, letters to attorneys—they fought from the outside while I battled from within. But with each small victory came harsh retaliation. Privileges vanished, solitary sentences piled up.

Other women began sharing their stories, each one stoking the fire in my belly. The chain of command swallowed misconduct reports without a ripple, protecting their own. We inmates had no rights, no recourse. Just trapped voices echoing in a void.

One sleepless night, I realized this wasn't just about me anymore. It was about every woman who'd been silenced, every injustice swept under the rug. I'd found a purpose beyond mere survival: to be a voice for the voiceless. And even if I couldn't win this fight, I'd at least make damn sure that the prison leadership knew they'd been in one.

The next morning, as I was released from solitary, I made a decision: Fred had to be stopped. And I might be the only one willing to take him on.

My eyes followed Fred's every move for weeks. I needed a witness, someone who couldn't be dismissed or intimidated. The opportunity came with a package from home: my contact lens solution.

As I approached the property room, I spotted a case worker—a man known for his strict adherence to rules—heading our way. My heart raced as a plan formed.

I pushed the door open, leaving it slightly ajar. Fred's voice carried clearly: "Here's your package. Is there anything I get for it?"

"You absolutely do," I purred, forcing a sultry tone. As Fred pressed against me, I angled myself to ensure the case worker had a clear view.

Gotcha, Fred.

Minutes later, I sat in the warden's office, surrounded by stern-faced officials.

"Officer Fred kissed me without my consent and groped me in the property room doorway," I stated, my voice steady despite my trembling hands.

Fred's face reddened. "She's lying!" he sputtered. "Just being manipulative. Everyone knows what a manipulator she is!"

The familiar clang of the solitary cell door echoed behind me, but this time, it felt different. I'd requested a PSE—a stress test designed to detect lies. I passed.

Thirty days later, I emerged to whispers of Fred's "early retirement." As I walked through the common area, I noticed a change. Women stood a little straighter, their eyes a bit brighter. Fred's victims could finally breathe easier. The system had fought back hard, but for once, it hadn't won.

CHAPTER 14

Better

The hum of washing machines filled the air as I folded sheets with Helen, another lifer who'd become a friend.

"Battered woman? What does that even mean?" I asked, my voice casual despite the sudden tightness in my chest.

Helen paused, smoothing a crease in a shirt. "It's about women who've been beaten—physically, sexually, emotionally. How the abuse changes your brain."

I flinched at the word *abuse*. That seemed too extreme. Sure, Charlie got out of control when drunk, but he loved me...right?

"There's a talk about it tonight," Helen continued. "You should come."

That evening, I sat in the back row, arms crossed defensively, as Dr. Lenore Walker took the stage. Her words pierced through my carefully constructed walls.

"Gaslighting," she explained, "is when an abuser denies reality, making the victim question their own sanity."

Charlie's voice echoed in my memory. "What bruises? You're imagining things, Judy."

Dr. Walker described cycles of abuse—tension building, explosion, honeymoon phase. My stomach churned as I recognized the pattern. Charlie's fists landing on my body—followed by tearful apologies. The time he threw a hot pan at me for cooking hot dogs—he hated hot dogs, why didn't I remember that?—followed by flowers and remorse.

"Trauma bonding," she continued, "occurs when pain is followed by comfort when the victim is most vulnerable."

Images flashed through my mind. Charlie holding me after a beating, whispering how much he loved me.

As Dr. Walker described the cycles of abuse and trauma, nausea rose in my throat. *Me too*, I realized with horror. *That's my life you're describing.* It was like Pavlov's dogs drooling at the bell—abuse was my bell, fear my conditioned response.

After the talk, I retreated to my cell, mind reeling. My inner world lay in ruins, a lifetime of beliefs shattered. Surrounded by concrete walls and iron bars, I felt more exposed than ever before. The prison that held my body suddenly seemed less confining than the one I'd built in my own mind.

The stories of other women echoed in my head—women begging for permission to visit family, having wallets and keys hidden from them. Their experiences were different from mine, yet the underlying pain was familiar.

What resonated most was my own involuntary flinch when a man raised his voice. That flinch was mine, a physical reminder of the fear Charlie had instilled in me. I couldn't control it, even years after leaving him.

After the talk, I hid in my cell, mind reeling. My inner world lay in ruins, a lifetime of beliefs shattered. I felt I didn't know even the most basic truths about myself anymore.

The realization that I was a battered woman didn't end with that talk. It was just the beginning.

A battered women's group from St. Louis visited monthly, holding open talks for inmates like me. One afternoon, I found myself sitting in a circle of women, my hands shaking slightly as I listened to their stories. The room smelled of stale coffee and disinfectant, but the air was clearer than I'd felt in years.

"Would you like to share, Judy?" the group leader asked gently.

I took a deep breath, surprised to hear my own voice. "It...it didn't start with my husband," I began, the words tumbling out. "It started with my dad."

As I spoke, memories I'd long buried resurfaced. The sound of my dad's heavy footsteps. The crack of his hand against my cheek. The suffocating silence that followed, when no one dared breathe too loudly.

Then came Charlie, my husband. I found myself telling them about the party at his friend's house. I could almost smell the beer and cigarette smoke as I described walking into the kitchen for a drink.

"I never heard him coming," I said, my voice barely above a whisper. "His hand slammed into the back of my head before I could turn. Then he grabbed my shoulders, slamming me backward."

I touched the back of my head unconsciously, feeling the old scar hidden beneath my hair. "My skull cracked against a cabinet. The room was spinning, and Charlie was bellowing in my face, 'Who were you talking to?!' "

The women around me listened, their faces a mix of understanding and sorrow. I told them about the host who tried to intervene, about Charlie hurrying me home, about spending the night pressing bloody rags to my throbbing head.

"I was terrified," I admitted. "But I had nowhere to turn. In our era, this was just... marital business. Not for outsiders to interfere."

As I finished speaking, a silence fell over the room. Then, slowly, other women began to share their own stories. I realized I wasn't alone in my experiences, in my shame, in my fear.

For years after, I'd traced that scar daily, a private reminder of the violence I'd endured. Now, in prison of all places, I was finally breaking the silence. As I listened to the other women, I felt something shift inside me. The shame that had weighed me down for so long began to lift, replaced by a growing sense of solidarity and strength.

The group sessions continued, and slowly, I began to understand my life for what it was: a tangled mess of hurt and bad habits. We did exercises that made me face things I'd been running from for decades. Every week, I felt a little lighter, like I was finally able to breathe after holding my breath for years.

The counselors taught me words for things I'd always felt but never understood: self-blame, codependency, traumatic bonding. We mapped out the cycle I'd been stuck in: tension, explosion, honeymoon phase, repeat.

Between sessions, I devoured anything that might help: Bible verses, meditation guides, psychology books. I filled notebooks, trying to untangle the mess in my head. Looking back with clear eyes, I finally understood why I'd done the things I'd done. I mourned for the girl I used to be, trapped by fear when a little kindness could have set her free.

Of course, seeing things clearly came with its own problems. Some days, the anger and bitterness nearly ate me alive. The guards' meanness, the endless red tape, missing my kids growing up—it was enough to make a person go crazy.

It was during one of these bitter moments that I came up with a new saying: "Don't be bitter; be better." I started saying it like a mantra.

When a guard made a snide comment, I'd take a deep breath. Don't be bitter; be better.

When I missed another of Angel's birthdays, I'd close my eyes and repeat it. Don't be bitter; be better.

It wasn't easy. Some days, the words felt hollow. But slowly, surely, the mantra clicked. I started to see my life like it was happening to someone else, and finally let go of the blame and shame and anger. I had to, or it would've destroyed me.

Becoming the best version of myself—that became my mission. It was the real way to get back at everyone who'd done me wrong. And with each passing day, with each repetition of my new mantra, I started to believe it. *Don't be bitter; be better.*

CHAPTER 15

Breath

As I walked down the corridor to the warden's office, the air heavy with tension, I could feel the guards' eyes on me. Their smirks told me this wasn't going to be good news.

The warden's voice was cold as he delivered the blow. "Henderson, you're being transferred. Interstate compact to Arizona." The Fred incident had been the final straw, prompting them to ship me off to a notorious maximum-security complex in Arizona, a facility with some of the nation's most dangerous criminals.

The words hit me like a physical force. Arizona. A thousand miles away. My mind reeled, grasping for understanding.

"But...my family," I stammered, my voice barely above a whisper. "My kids..."

The warden's face remained impassive. "You should have thought about that before you caused so much trouble here."

As I stumbled back to my cell, the full weight of the

situation set in. No more visits from my children. No more of my mother's desperate efforts to support me. The threads connecting me to the outside world, already frayed, would finally snap.

Even in solitary at Renz Farm, I could find solace in breathing the same Missouri air as my loved ones. But Arizona? It might as well have been Mars.

That night, I paced my small cell, my mind racing. I could almost hear the administration's thoughts: *Let's see how this suburban mom fares in the big leagues.* To them, it was a perfect solution: One way or another, I'd no longer be their problem.

As dawn broke, I stood at my tiny window, watching the familiar Missouri landscape. Soon, this view would be replaced by unforgiving desert. The faces I'd come to know—fellow inmates, even the guards I'd battled—would be replaced by strangers.

In the eyes of those who'd once known Judy Henderson, I would fade into a ghost—out of sight and, inevitably, out of mind. The thought was more suffocating than any isolation cell.

The clanking of my chains echoed through the bustling St. Louis airport. Each step was a struggle, the shackles that chained my legs together forcing an awkward shuffle. I kept my eyes fixed on the floor, but I could feel the stares burning into me.

"Mommy, why is that lady wearing those things?" A child's voice pierced the air.

"Don't look, sweetie," came the hushed reply.

A group of teenagers snickered as we passed. "Wonder what she did," one whispered loudly.

My face burned with shame I knew I didn't deserve. The guard's grip on my arm tightened as we approached security.

"Bathroom break," she grunted.

The women's restroom fell silent as we entered. I could feel the shock emanating from the other stalls as the guard followed me in, the handcuffs between us clanking against the metal partition.

"Can you..." I started, my voice barely audible.

"You know the rules," she cut me off.

Struggling with my restraints, I managed the basic task, acutely aware of the judgment from neighboring stalls. As we exited, a mother pulled her young daughter close, eyeing me warily.

On the plane, I stared at the empty seat beside me. Another officer sat in the aisle seat, and another sat behind me. Whispers floated from nearby rows.

"What do you think she did?"

"Must be something terrible."

I pressed my forehead against the cool window as the plane took off. The Missouri landscape shrank below, a patchwork of green and brown. Somewhere down there, my children were going about their day. Were they looking up at this very plane, imagining their mother waving back?

"Angel, Chip," I whispered, my breath fogging the glass. "Momma loves you."

As we crossed into Arizona, the view changed to endless

desert. My hopes felt just as barren. I was heading into the unknown, leaving behind everything and everyone I loved.

A tear slid down my cheek. The guard pretended not to notice.

As the plane began its descent into this alien landscape, I closed my eyes. In that moment, suspended between the sky and the earth, I'd never felt so alone.

The Santa Maria Unit loomed in the barren Arizona desert, a fortress of concrete and steel. As our bus rattled through the imposing gates, I felt a chill. This desolate place would be my new home.

Inside, the process of dehumanization began immediately. "Strip," a guard barked. I hesitated, then slowly complied, feeling exposed and vulnerable. They deloused us like cattle, then handed out our new uniforms.

The shoes caught my attention—flimsy canvas sneakers with a crude *V* cut from each heel.

"So we can track you if you run," a guard explained coldly. "The print stands out in the sand."

I stared at those mutilated shoes, a pit forming in my stomach. To them, we were just animals to be hunted if we strayed.

My resolve faced a brutal test in those first days. Not long after arriving at my assigned pod, a hard-eyed Hispanic inmate approached me.

"You want some chiva?" she asked.

I blinked, uncomprehending. "No. What's chiva?"

"Heroin," she replied with a knowing smirk.

Later, my cellmate stumbled in, reeking of alcohol.

"How do you get alcohol in here?" I whispered. She just tapped her nose, a sly grin on her lips.

I quickly learned that drugs permeated every corner of Santa Maria Unit. Care packages were Trojan horses—popcorn concealing oxycontin, letters laced with meth. Heroin, cocaine, LSD—all smuggled in under stamps, inside tennis balls, even within inmates' bodies.

The outdoor track became a staging ground for drug use. As we circled endlessly, I noticed women slipping away, vomiting quietly in the shadows.

"You puke to get higher," someone explained matter-of-factly when I asked.

It was the rocks that truly welcomed me to Arizona prison life—endless piles of them, baking under the merciless desert sun. They called it "orientation," but it felt more like punishment.

Every morning, we'd file out to the track, a miles-long loop encircling the prison yard. Our job? To rake rocks from one side of the track to the other. Hour after hour, day after day.

The sun beat down relentlessly, turning the air into a shimmering haze. Sweat poured down my face, soaking my clothes within minutes. Water was scarce, and the guards seemed unconcerned with our thirst or exhaustion.

I watched as some women swayed on their feet, dizzy from dehydration. A few even collapsed, their bodies giving out under the strain. The guards would have them sit for a bit, then expect them back at it.

As I struggled to keep my footing on the shifting gravel, my thoughts drifted to the cool Missouri air I imagined I'd never see again. But I gritted my teeth and kept raking. I'd survived worse than this, I told myself. I'd survived Charlie's fists, Greg's betrayal, and the injustice of my sentencing. I could survive this too.

On my darkest days, I counted time in tiny bits—five minutes of raking, then a couple of breaths of stolen rest. One page of reading, then thinking. A single lap walking the edge. Baby steps taken day after day, year after year, became miles.

They had taken my freedom, my identity, even my shoes. But some things remained beyond their reach. I was no longer the scared "new fish" who'd entered Renz Farm. They could track my steps, but not my spirit. They could mark my heel, but not extinguish the fire in my mind.

The Santa Maria Unit was a study in contradictions. The inmates here were more violent, more ruthless than any I'd known in Missouri. Every day felt like walking a tightrope over a pit of vipers. Yet, paradoxically, this harsh environment offered something Missouri never could: real rehabilitation.

Arizona's deeper pockets showed in their approach to inmate care. While Missouri struggled to provide basic necessities, Arizona had the resources for comprehensive programs. It was a bitter irony: I had to be transferred to a more dangerous prison to access the help I'd needed all along.

Back at Renz Farm, the battered women's group therapy had been helpful, but individual counseling was a joke—a way to keep us docile with psychotropic drugs. We called it "the Thorazine shuffle," watching fellow inmates stumble through days in a drooling stupor. I'd refused to join that sad parade, knowing it'd only leave me more vulnerable.

Arizona was different. Here the counselors were clear, focused, genuinely interested in my well-being. No haze of drugs, no shuffling zombies—just real, one-on-one therapy.

The differences showed when I stepped into my first therapy session. "Tell me about your childhood, Judy," she said, her voice gentle but firm.

I hesitated, memories I'd long buried threatening to surface. "I...I don't know where to start."

"Start anywhere," she encouraged. "We've got time."

Twice a week, we'd meet in a plain room, its walls a neutral beige. Over time, those walls became witnesses to my deepest confessions.

"I used to write apologies to my father," I admitted one day, my voice barely above a whisper. "After he'd beat me. I'd slip them on his pillow, begging forgiveness for...for making him angry."

The counselor's face remained calm, but I saw a flicker of pain in her eyes. "And how do you feel about that now?"

It was a simple question, but it cracked something open inside me. Suddenly, I was sobbing, years of pent-up grief pouring out.

As weeks turned to months, we peeled back layers of

trauma. Childhood abuse at the hands of a relative and the assistant pastor. The violence in my marriage to Charlie. The manipulation by Greg that led me here.

"I should have known better," I said during one session, frustration coloring my voice. "I should have seen the red flags with Greg."

"Judy," the counselor leaned forward, her gaze intent. "You're not responsible for other people's actions. You did nothing to deserve any of this."

It was a line I'd heard before, but never truly believed until that moment.

These sessions left me raw, exposed. Some nights, sleep was impossible, my mind racing with newfound realizations. But I knew this was the only way forward—I had to face the past to have any shot at a future.

We tackled my codependency, how I'd become addicted to the idea of love. "You've been relying on others for happiness, for purpose," she explained. "But true contentment can only come from within."

As I grappled with these revelations, I felt a shift. I was becoming empowered, learning to make choices based on my own needs, not others' expectations. I discovered a strength I never knew I had.

"I'm more than my traumas," I said during one session, surprising myself with the conviction in my voice. "More than tough choices made in fear."

The counselor smiled. "Yes, you are. You're a survivor, Judy. A victor."

In that sterile prison room, I found a freedom no court could grant me. The real chains weren't the ones on my wrists, but the ones in my mind. And for the first time, I felt them start to break.

When not in counseling, I lost myself in books. The Arizona prison library became my sanctuary, a far cry from Missouri's meager offerings. Each evening after dinner, I'd make my way there, the familiar scent of old books welcoming me like an old friend.

"Back again, Henderson?" the librarian would say with a knowing smile.

I'd nod, already scanning the shelves for my next escape.

This library was more than books—it was the raw material to rebuild my shattered self. I devoured anything on psychology, spirituality, philosophy, religion—anything that could help me make sense of my broken world.

Dr. Lenore Walker's *The Battered Woman Syndrome* felt like looking into a mirror. As I read, I found myself nodding, tears stinging my eyes. Finally, someone understood.

Wayne Dyer's *Your Erroneous Zones* became my constant companion, dog-eared and worn. Rick Warren's *The Purpose Driven Life* and Kahlil Gibran's *The Prophet* took turns on my table, their words a light in the darkness. Maya Angelou's fierce resilience and Joyce Meyer's transformation from abuse victim to spiritual leader showed me what was possible.

One day, I stumbled upon Joel Osteen's *Your Best Life Now*. His message of positivity and self-improvement resonated with me, even as I struggled with the irony of reading about my "best life" while behind bars.

"You planning on preaching, Henderson?" a guard once quipped, eyeing the stack of spiritual books in my arms.

I managed a small smile. "Just trying to find my way."

Nelson Mandela's *Long Walk to Freedom* hit close to home. His rural childhood was so like my own, and his decades behind bars gave me a glimmer of hope. If he could emerge from that crucible without bitterness, maybe I could too.

In those books, I found an escape from my cell, a way to travel beyond these walls. I explored new ideas, new perspectives, finding kindred spirits in authors I'd never meet.

In that library, surrounded by other stories of overcoming, I began to see my own life differently. Maybe my story wasn't over. Maybe I could write a new chapter—one of strength, of resilience, of hope.

CHAPTER 16

Mindful

The chapel at Renz Farm in Missouri had been a turning point. During the Residents Encounter Christ program, I'd felt a flicker of hope that there might be some divine plan behind all this pain. But here in Arizona, that hope wavered.

One Sunday, I found myself in the prison chapel, Bible in hand. The familiar hymns washed over me, but something felt off. I couldn't shake the feeling that I was going through the motions, mouthing words that no longer held meaning.

"You okay, Henderson?" whispered the inmate next to me, noticing my distraction.

I nodded, forcing a smile. But inside, I was wrestling with doubts I'd never dared voice before.

The next day, I headed to the library, drawn to the shelves I'd always avoided before. My fingers traced the spines of books on Eastern philosophy, world religions, spirituality.

"Broadening your horizons?" the librarian asked, eyebrow raised as I checked out a stack of Buddhist texts.

I shrugged. "Just...exploring." This wasn't about turning my back on Christianity; it was about understanding how others saw the divine.

That night, I cracked open *The Miracle of Mindfulness* by Thich Nhat Hanh. As I read about mindfulness and inner peace, something resonated deep within me. Here was a path that said "Look within," that the answers were already inside me.

Studying peace in a maximum-security prison felt like planting flowers in a war zone. But these Buddhist teachings gave me purpose in a place designed to strip it away. Buddha's words became my mantra: "Hatred does not cease by hatred, but only by love."

One afternoon, during yard time, I found a quiet corner and tried to meditate. Closing my eyes, I focused on my breath, just as the books had described. For a few moments, the noise of the prison faded away. When I opened my eyes, the world seemed a little brighter.

Mindfulness meditation became my secret weapon against an unruly mind. When memories ambushed me or panic squeezed tight, I'd focus on my breath—in and out, steady as a metronome. Watching each breath, I found space between trigger and response. My thoughts no longer ran wild like spooked horses.

I started a notebook, scribbling down insights and teachings. It became my homemade survival guide. Some days, the teachings felt like revelation. Others, they were cold comfort against harsh reality. But that wisdom kept me afloat in the darkest waters.

As I practiced, I discovered a profound truth: My body might be locked up, but my mind—my spirit—was learning to soar beyond these walls. Simple pleasures became profound: warm water on skin; laughter with fellow inmates; a single sunbeam painting gold on concrete.

In my bunk at night, I'd still whisper prayers to the God of my childhood. But now, I also practiced mindfulness, seeking that inner calm the Buddhist texts described.

It wasn't neat or tidy, didn't fit in any one box. But in this place where so much had been taken from me, having a faith that was truly my own felt like the most precious freedom of all.

The thing that surprised me most about Arizona's prison wasn't the oppressive heat or the more violent inmates—it was the sense of purpose that seemed to hum through the air. Unlike the stagnant atmosphere of Missouri's Renz Farm, where inmates festered in a vacuum of meaningless routine, Arizona felt...alive.

Despite housing some of the nation's most dangerous offenders, this place pulsed with an unexpected energy. Rehabilitation wasn't just a buzzword here; it was a tangible force. Every day brought new programs, therapies, and educational opportunities.

We weren't just passing time—we were being offered a chance to grow, to heal, to become more than the sum of our worst decisions. For a woman who'd spent years believing her life was over, this was nothing short of revolutionary. I threw myself into every opportunity, hungry for change, for meaning.

But amid the structured programs and counseling sessions,

I stumbled upon something I never expected to find in a maximum-security prison—a connection to an ancient spiritual lineage as vast and enduring as the Arizona desert itself.

It began with a simple invitation from a Native American inmate with eyes that seemed to hold centuries of wisdom. "We're having a spiritual circle tonight," she said, her voice low and steady. "Would you like to join us?"

I nodded, both excited and nervous. That evening, I entered the circle like a skittish colt, smoothing my clothes anxiously. The other women's eyes were kind but neutral, making space without fuss.

The leader lit a bundle of sage. Its smoke curled around us like a living thing. "For purification," she murmured, brushing a feathered wand over me. I shivered as an unseen weight seemed to lift from my spirit.

Then came the chant. Strange sounds repeated over and over, until I found myself falling into rhythm with the others. My racing thoughts slowed, then stilled. That steady chant anchored me in the present, keeping painful memories at bay.

Afterward, we shared our burdens. These women listened without judgment, offering advice or just silent compassion. In their eyes, I saw a reflection of light I'd forgotten was in me.

I kept going back, drawn to these timeless traditions. We held talking circles under the vast desert sky, passing an eagle feather to speak our truths. At powwows, I savored buffalo stew and fry bread, dancing with a pride I thought I'd lost.

In Arizona's harsh desert, I found what I'd been searching

for my whole life. These Native practices gave me a sense of connection that even prison bars couldn't contain. It was like finding an oasis in the middle of a wasteland— unexpected, precious, life-giving.

For the first time since I'd been locked up, I felt part of something bigger than myself. I was not just a number, not just an inmate, but a human being connected to an ancient lineage of wisdom and strength.

The lights buzzed overhead as I stared at the GED program flyer. My fingers traced the words, a mix of excitement and fear churning in my stomach.

"You thinking of signing up?" a fellow inmate asked.

I nodded, not trusting my voice. Education was a door I'd thought forever sealed after the assistant pastor's attack derailed my high school years. Instead of algebra and literature, I'd learned the brutal arithmetic of supporting a family on long hours and low wages.

The first day of class, I clutched my borrowed textbook like a life preserver. As the teacher dove into fractions, my mind creaked and groaned under the strain.

"This is impossible," I muttered, eraser shavings piling up on my desk.

"Keep at it," my seatmate encouraged. "It gets easier."

Late nights in my cell, I pored over practice problems by the dim light allowed after lights-out. Slowly, the fog began to lift. Sentences sharpened into focus, equations clicked into place, and the gears of my mind, neglected for so long, began to turn once more.

The day of the GED exam arrived. My hands shook as I filled in the answer bubbles.

"Time's up," the proctor announced. I let out a breath I didn't know I'd been holding.

Weeks later, I found out I passed. Tears stung my eyes as I stared at my scores. At last, I was a high school graduate.

Buoyed by this success, I dove into every community college course available. My schedule became a patchwork of classes: Sociology on Mondays, Psychology on Tuesdays, Government on Wednesdays.

"You're taking on quite a load," my counselor remarked, eyebrow raised.

I shrugged. "I've got time," I replied, a wry smile playing on my lips.

As I aced assignments and racked up strong grades, I realized I was doing more than making up for lost time. Each perfect score, each "A" paper, was a building block in a new foundation.

One day, reviewing my transcript, I gasped. A perfect 4.0 GPA stared back at me.

"Everything okay?" another inmate asked, concerned.

I nodded, unable to speak past the lump in my throat. This wasn't just a number. It was proof that even in the unlikeliest of places, transformation was possible.

As I stood before the warden, my heart was racing. "I want to start a support group," I said, my voice steadier than I felt. "For domestic violence survivors."

The warden's eyebrow arched. "In prison?"

I nodded, thinking of the hidden bruises I'd seen on so many women here. "We need this," I insisted.

After a moment's hesitation, he gave his nod. Women Against Violence (WAV) was born.

Our first meeting, I stood before a room of wary faces. "I've been where you are," I began, my voice catching. "But we're not victims anymore. We're survivors."

Slowly, women began to share their stories. Tears flowed, but so did strength. We practiced assertiveness, role-playing scenarios that once would have terrified us.

"No," Maria said firmly, her chin lifted as she faced her imaginary abuser. "I deserve better."

The room erupted in applause.

Word spread. Officials started dropping in on our sessions, amazed at the transformation they witnessed. Even the governor took notice, sparking a task force on domestic violence.

As WAV grew, so did I. People saw leadership in me—a notion that once would've made me scoff. I became a beacon in the prison, sought out by women needing guidance or just a friendly ear.

It was during this time that the prison decided to shake things up with a bit of showbiz. A local production company swept in, bringing song, dance, and laughter to our drab world.

"Henderson," the recreation director called out one day. "They want you to learn some dances, teach the other women."

Before I knew it, I was leading impromptu dance lessons across the prison yard. The Charleston, the Mashed Potato, the Bus Stop—we did them all.

"Cross your feet, then pivot," I instructed, demonstrating the Charleston. At first, I stumbled, my knees knocking like a newborn colt's. But gradually, the moves flowed into that iconic swaying strut.

For Motown numbers, we strutted and shimmied, channeling the Supremes. "Stop! In the name of love," we sang, striking dramatic poses.

As we laughed and stumbled through steps, we weren't numbered prisoners anymore—just giddy girls again. When the big show arrived, we sparkled under makeshift stage lights, moving as one while waves of applause washed over us.

That night, as I hung up my costume, I realized something profound. Through WAV and these dance lessons, I'd found more than just purpose. I'd rediscovered joy.

As the spotlight faded, a whirlwind of emotions swept over me. The show's thrill, our collective pride, the bond with my fellow inmates—it all crashed against the hard truth of my circumstances. There I stood, in a prison that offered chances I'd never imagined, yet I felt more isolated than ever.

"Great job tonight, Henderson," a guard said as I walked back to my cell.

I nodded, forcing a smile. But inside, I was screaming. Angel was celebrating another birthday next week, and I'd be missing it. Again.

In Missouri, I'd seen her twice a month. Now, in this land of opportunity, those precious moments had shrunk to twice a year. The irony was bitter—I was healing, learning, even flourishing in some ways, but at what cost?

That night, I stared at the ceiling, wondering about the small moments I was missing. Did Angel still lose herself in books? Did she remember the stories I used to weave at bedtime?

The next morning, I dragged myself to the Long-Timers group meeting. As I listened to other mothers share their pain of separation, an idea began to form.

"What if we did something for the kids?" I suggested, my voice hesitant. "For the holidays?"

The room fell silent, then erupted in excited chatter.

Over the next weeks, we transformed the visiting room. For Halloween, we hung crepe paper and mixed face paint. At Christmas, we crafted handmade gifts.

"Mommy, look!" a little boy squealed, showing off his painted face. His mother's eyes shone with tears of joy.

Each visit I witnessed was a bittersweet reminder of what I'd lost. But in helping others, I found a way to channel my grief into purpose.

We organized letter-writing campaigns for inmates who struggled with literacy. I sat with a fellow inmate-mother, helping her pen a letter to her son.

"Tell him about your day," I encouraged. "The little things matter."

As she wrote, I thought of my own letters to Angel, filled with questions I feared might never be answered.

We spread the word about weekend visit programs and assembled care packages. One afternoon, as I packed a box with shampoo, notebooks, and candy bars, another inmate approached.

"Henderson," she said softly, "thank you. My daughter loved the gift I made her last Christmas."

I blinked back tears, nodding. As I focused on others, my self-pity began to recede like the Arizona horizon. I couldn't bridge the distance to my own children, but I could help other mothers maintain their precious connections.

That night, as I penned another letter to Angel, I realized a profound truth: Our deepest healing often comes through service to others. In easing the pain of fellow inmates, I'd found a balm for my own wounds, a way to give meaning to my suffering.

No, I couldn't be there to guide Angel through adolescence, but I could show her—through my actions, even from afar—the power of resilience and compassion. And maybe, just maybe, that was the most important lesson a mother could teach.

CHAPTER 17

Snake Charmer

One of Arizona's finest blessings came when I met Cathy, a lifer we fondly called Butch. With her tattooed arms and tough exterior, she seemed an unlikely source of wisdom. Yet it was Butch who would teach me that conquering fear was about facing our demons head-on.

"With anything in life, if you're afraid of it, you have to face the fear and do it anyway," Butch told me one day, her tattooed arms crossed.

I nodded, not realizing how soon I'd be putting that advice to the test.

In Arizona, snakes were everywhere, often slithering into cells and showers. My fear of them was paralyzing. That's when Butch prescribed her unique brand of therapy: snake exposure.

"Just trust me," Butch said, holding out a baby snake. "Let it crawl."

I closed my eyes, heart pounding as the snake glided over my gloved hands. Gradually, I could open my eyes.

Then I was able to shed the gloves, acclimating to the smooth, scaly sensation on bare skin.

Weeks passed, and my confidence grew. Soon, I was draping larger snakes around my neck, channeling Cleopatra. I even adopted a pet snake, which I named Mariah. Butch had transformed my snake-induced panic into a sense of empowerment.

This newfound skill led to one of my most amusing Arizona memories. One night, an officer passing my cell noticed me putting something in my blouse.

"Henderson, I want to do a strip search," she demanded.

"You really don't want to do that..." I cautioned.

"Take it all off," she insisted.

As I lifted my shirt, Mariah's head emerged. The guard shrieked and bolted from the cell, yelling about a deadly viper.

"It's okay, don't be scared!" I called after her, chuckling.

As I gently placed Mariah back in her box, Butch's words echoed in my mind: face your fears and do it anyway.

I marveled at how far I'd come. From a woman terrified of snakes, I'd become the prison's unofficial snake charmer. I was finding ways to not just survive, but to thrive, learning lessons I never could have imagined on the outside.

But despite these small victories, a deep ache persisted. Arizona could never be home. Some siblings had moved near me in Arizona, but my children and my mother were back in Missouri. Any hope for redemption lay closer to them.

One April Fool's Day, that homesickness sparked an

ill-advised prank. I dialed my sister JoElla's number, my heart racing.

"Sis, listen," I said, my voice dead serious. "I've escaped. I'm at the station on the corner. I need you to pick me up."

A stunned silence followed. "What?! What did you say?!" JoElla stammered, her voice climbing an octave.

Minutes later, after revealing the joke, I exploded with laughter. "April Fool's!" I gasped between giggles.

JoElla's exasperated groan carried a mix of relief and annoyance. "Oh my God, Judy, you nearly gave me a heart attack!"

As our laughter faded, the reality of my situation settled back in. I was still here, still far from home.

About six months before I went to Arizona, I connected with a lawyer named Bob Ramsey. I met him when he visited another inmate, and knowing his work on criminal cases, I asked for an introduction.

"Your lawyer did not represent you according to the Constitution, Judy," Bob said after reviewing my case, his brow furrowed with concern.

From that moment, Bob became my advocate. He persistently pushed for my return to Missouri, proposing an inmate exchange.

"They're saying Missouri wants you permanently exiled," Bob told me during one of our phone calls. "But we're not giving up."

Year after year, Bob appealed their rejections. Bob would mail documents to me in Arizona, and we'd speak regularly over the phone.

"We're highlighting your GED, your counseling work, your volunteer efforts," he explained. "We're building an irrefutable case for your return."

Still, Missouri prison officials stood firm. But Bob's resolve never wavered.

After four grueling years, we prevailed. The day Bob told me to pack my bags, I wept with disbelief and relief.

As the bus pulled away from Arizona, I pressed my forehead against the cool window. "Thank you, Bob," I whispered. He was more than just a lawyer. He was a pillar of faith when mine faltered, a tireless champion who never lost belief in justice.

I was going home, back to Missouri, back to hope, and back to my family. And it was all because of Bob.

The plane touched down in St. Louis. "On your feet," the marshal ordered, unlocking my shackles.

I stumbled onto the tarmac, where two Fulton Prison officers waited. Their faces were stone, betraying no emotion as they led me to a van.

"Welcome home," one muttered, his voice dripping with sarcasm.

The drive to Fulton was silent. I pressed my forehead against the cool window, watching familiar landscapes blur past. After years in Arizona, even the Missouri trees seemed to welcome me back.

My homecoming fantasy shattered the moment we arrived at Fulton. Instead of processing, they marched me straight to solitary confinement.

"Wait, there must be some mistake," I protested as the cell door clanged shut.

The guard's eyes were cold. "No mistake, Henderson. Enjoy your stay."

Confusion gave way to anger as the days dragged on. I hadn't broken any rules. In Arizona, I'd been in the Honor Dorm—home to model inmates with clean records. Why this cruel welcome?

The truth trickled down through whispers and overheard conversations. My file was poisoned with lies.

"She's trouble," I heard one guard tell another. "A master manipulator. They exiled her for a reason."

The tiny, frigid cell felt like it was closing in on me. But I refused to break. Years inside had taught me the system's inner workings, and I used that knowledge as my shield.

When they accused me of fabricated infractions, I was ready. "The policy manual clearly states..." I'd begin, watching their faces fall as I cited exact rules.

For every unfair write-up, I filed a meticulous grievance. My pen became my weapon, documenting every misstep and violation.

"You can't intimidate me," I told a particularly aggressive guard one day. "I know my rights."

At night, I'd scribble detailed accounts to Bob Ramsey. My hand cramped as I filled page after page, but I knew Bob would read every word.

His response was swift and fierce. "This is outrageous and unlawful," he thundered over the phone to the warden. "Her record is unblemished. End this solitary confinement immediately."

Slowly, the tide began to turn. The unfair treatment

didn't stop entirely, but it became more subtle. They realized I wouldn't be an easy target.

As I lay on my thin mattress one night, I allowed myself a small smile. I was back in Missouri, closer to my family and to hope. The road ahead would be tough, but I was tougher. I'd fought my way back home, and I wasn't about to let anyone push me down again.

The cell door's creak had become my only companion. Twenty-eight days in solitary, the longest stretch I'd ever endured. I traced patterns on the wall, counting the hours until my next meal, my next breath of recycled air.

Then, on day twenty-nine, a new voice pierced the silence. "Henderson?"

I looked up to see an unfamiliar face peering through the small window in my door. The unit's supervising sergeant, back from vacation.

"Hi! How are you?" I chirped, my voice hoarse from disuse but genuinely glad for human interaction.

The sergeant's eyebrows shot up, surprise evident on her face. She'd clearly been expecting someone—or something—else.

Later, I learned about the conversation that followed. The sergeant, marching straight to the unit caseworker, demanded answers.

"I don't understand why she's still in the hole," she declared. "She doesn't belong down there."

The next day, my cell door opened. Not for a meal or a shower, but for good.

"Pack up, Henderson," a guard announced. "You're moving to general population."

The world beyond solitary was a sensory assault. Colors seemed too bright, voices too loud. Women bustled past, their movements a blur after weeks of stillness. In Arizona, our prison doors had opened to the outside, to fresh air and space. Here, the corridors felt claustrophobic.

I pressed my back against a wall, trying to steady my breathing. A passing inmate paused, concern etching her features.

"You okay, new girl?" she asked.

I nodded, managing a weak smile. "Just...adjusting."

She patted my arm. "It gets easier. Welcome to Fulton."

As I followed her to my new housing unit, I felt a mix of relief and apprehension. The isolation was over, but new challenges lay ahead. Malicious rumors had preceded me, painting me as a monster to be feared.

But I'd faced worse. I'd survived Arizona's heat, Missouri's cold shoulder, and nearly a month in the hole. This was just another hurdle to overcome. I would show them who I really was—not the monster they'd been told about, but the woman who'd fought her way back home.

One friendly "hello" at a time, I'd build a new community here. After all, I'd done it before. And this time, I was on home turf.

"Angel, honey, you need to boil the water before adding the sweet potatoes," I said into the phone, picturing my daughter's frustrated face on the other end.

"But Mom, it's taking forever!" Angel whined.

I chuckled, ignoring the ache in my chest. "Patience, sweetheart. Good things take time."

These phone calls sustained me, as I tried to distill a lifetime of motherly wisdom into fleeting conversations.

As Angel ventured into the world of first crushes and school dances, I fumbled to guide her, drawing from outdated TV shows and experiences I'd never had.

"Remember, a boy should treat you with respect," I told her one day, my voice firm despite the uncertainty I felt. How do you teach your daughter about love from behind bars?

When her first heartbreak came, all I could offer were words. "It hurts now, but it won't forever," I said, wishing I could hold her as she cried.

My family, bless them, always ensured I remained part of their story. At every gathering, they left an empty seat with my photograph. A poignant reminder of my spiritual, if not physical, presence.

But not everyone was so lucky. I saw other mothers struggling, their bonds with their children fraying under the strain of separation. One woman's story struck me hard. Her visits with her young son had dwindled to nothing, leaving her hollow-eyed and withdrawn.

That's when I remembered the PATCH program from Renz Farm. No barriers, no scrutiny—just cooking meals, playing games, sharing stories and laughter. I approached the officials at Fulton with the idea.

"It'll improve behavior and morale," I argued. They agreed to a trial run.

The transformation was almost immediate. On visiting

days, the dreary yard sprang to life with children's laughter. I watched as hardened faces softened, mothers doting on their little ones with a joy I recognized all too well.

Word spread quickly. Soon, we had a waiting list of mothers eager to participate. It wasn't enough—it could never be enough—but it was something.

The sergeant who freed me from solitary soon asked me to address an international Methodist conference by phone from her office. Speaking to a global audience, I conveyed incarcerated women's desperate longing to reconnect with their families.

"The PATCH program is important," I told attendees worldwide. "It represents hope that our children haven't forgotten us, that our love still reaches them. Without it, many women would suffer. But with your support, bonds can be preserved..."

Standing in the PATCH trailer one day, surrounded by the sounds of families reconnecting, I closed my eyes and smiled. This was my legacy. Not the crime that brought me here, but the love and hope I'd helped nurture in this unlikely place.

Individual programs were one thing. But in prison, I learned—and witnessed—how whole systems could be changed, too.

Our stories, our struggles, our pain—they had power beyond the prison walls. They could touch hearts, open minds, and even change laws. I saw this firsthand one unforgettable morning, when lawmakers made the unprecedented decision to visit us, to hear directly from the women whose lives their laws had shaped.

The room fell silent as I stepped up to speak. Legislators, inmates, and advocates leaned forward, their eyes fixed on me.

"I stand before you not just as an inmate," I began, my voice steadier than I felt, "but as a survivor of domestic abuse."

I took a deep breath, remembering the countless women who couldn't be here to speak for themselves.

"Imagine living in constant fear," I continued. "Imagine bracing for the next attack, barely holding yourself together. That was my reality. That is the reality for many women behind these walls."

As I spoke, I saw faces change. Skepticism gave way to shock, then to empathy. One senator wiped away a tear.

"Abuse becomes your normal," I said, my voice cracking slightly. "Your only focus is survival. And sometimes, that survival means fighting back."

After my speech, other survivors stepped forward. Their trembling voices filled the room with stories of terror, of helplessness, of desperate acts of self-defense that landed them in prison.

Months of advocacy had led to this moment. We had achieved the unprecedented—lawmakers visiting the prison, hearing our stories firsthand.

As the last woman finished speaking, a hush fell over the room. Then, a legislator stood up.

"Thank you," he said, his voice thick with emotion. "We...we had no idea."

In the weeks that followed, I spoke to three media outlets, determined to keep the momentum going.

"The public needs to understand," I told a reporter, "how broken laws trap countless women in cycles of violence."

The day the law passed—unanimously, recognizing battered woman syndrome as a legal defense—I sat in my cell, overwhelmed with emotion.

"We did it," I whispered to my cellmate, who had also testified. "We actually did it."

It was a bittersweet victory. Many of my friends would never leave these walls. But for future abuse victims, we had carved out a slim chance at justice.

As news of our success spread, I received letters from lawmakers in other states, seeking advice on similar reforms. We might be behind bars, but our voices could still stir consciences and effect change. And that, perhaps, was the greatest freedom of all.

"Miss Judy!" A young inmate's voice pulled me from my thoughts. "Can you help me with something?"

I turned, smiling. "Of course, honey. What do you need?"

As I listened to her concerns, offering gentle advice, I marveled at how natural this felt now. The nervous, broken Judy Henderson who'd first arrived in prison seemed like a distant memory.

Later that day, as I walked across the yard, I noticed the subtle nods of respect from longtime inmates. My stride was purposeful, my head held high.

I remember a middle-aged woman standing in the prison hallway, looking lost.

"Excuse me, ma'am," she began, eyeing my neat appearance. "Could you tell me where to find the visiting room?"

"Of course," I smiled. "I'd be happy to show you. I'm Judy, by the way."

"Oh, thank goodness," she sighed with relief. "I've been looking everywhere. Are you a counselor here?"

I paused, considering my words carefully. "No, ma'am. I'm an inmate. But I've been here long enough to know my way around."

The surprise on her face was familiar, but it no longer bothered me. To the prison community, I was "Miss Judy" or "the Governor," revered for my protective wisdom. This unofficial authority, born of respect rather than rank, had become a source of quiet pride.

As she walked away, I recalled the small piece of paper tucked above my mirror—a quote from Jeremiah 29:11. "'For I know the plans I have for you,' declares the LORD, 'plans to prosper you and not to harm you, plans to give you hope and a future.'" Those words had taken on new meaning for me over the years.

The world might still judge me, but their labels could no longer diminish the worth I'd discovered within. I had become someone inmates naturally sought for guidance and fairness—and more importantly, someone I could respect when I looked in the mirror.

PART III

CHAPTER 18

I Got This

In December 1990, all women were transferred from Fulton back to Renz Farm. Then, in 1993, a devastating flood forced us to relocate. For a brief period, we were crammed like sardines into a gym inside a men's prison. Finally, we settled at Chillicothe Correctional Center, which would become my home for the remainder of my sentence.

As the floodwaters receded, a new threat emerged. Missouri appointed a harsh new warden to Chillicothe, a man who scoffed at rehabilitation. In his cold eyes, we deserved nothing but punishment.

His first decree stripped away our washing machines and dryers. For the next two grueling years, we washed clothes, sheets, and rugs by hand in five-gallon buckets.

At first, it seemed like a mere inconvenience. But as days stretched into months, the physical toll became unbearable. Our knuckles cracked and bled from hours of scrubbing and wringing.

This was just the beginning. The warden doled out arbi-
trary punishments, creating an atmosphere of constant
fear. A heavy gloom settled over the prison. He seemed
determined to crush any spark of hope among us.

Then, the suicides began. It started with a few women
who couldn't take it anymore. They made nooses from torn
sheets, hanging themselves from cell bars at night. Another
climbed the fire escape and used her sheet there.

These deaths shocked everyone, but the idea of escape
through death spread quickly. Soon, the sound of running
guards became common, their keys jangling as they rushed
to cut down another inmate before it was too late.

One memory still haunts me: the burial of a lifer who
finally ended her life. She was my cellmate once. We'd
spent hours together, and now she was gone. With no family left, the prison buried her in an unmarked plot. A pastor
simply said a few quick words over her grave, and that was
that.

At night, we heard screams of despair. The days brought
no relief, just more backbreaking work. Something had to
be done.

The rebellion started as a whisper in the yard. "We
need to fight back," an inmate murmured, her eyes darting
around to check for guards. "A protest."

Within days, a plan had formed: We would refuse to eat
in the dining hall. It wasn't quite a hunger strike, but it
would send a clear message.

I wasn't an organizer, but I knew about the plan. When

the first meal came, dozens of women stayed in their cells. The clatter of trays in the dining hall was eerily quiet.

It didn't take long for the warden to react. That afternoon, an officer escorted me to his office without explanation. I steeled myself as we crossed the street, silently praying for courage.

The warden's face was a mask of fury as he glared at me from behind his desk. "I've got one question for you, Henderson," he snapped. "Who is responsible for this food strike nonsense?"

I met his gaze steadily. "I don't know who is responsible, sir."

His fist slammed down on the desk. "I'm going to ask you one more time!" he snarled. "Give me the name of the woman who started this, or you'll be sorry."

I stood my ground. "Like I said, I don't know what you're talking about."

Shaking with rage, the warden leaned forward. "Here's what's going to happen. You're going back across the street, and you're going to write down the names of the people behind the food strike. If you don't tell me who's responsible, I'll bury you so deep that even your fancy political friends like Dale Whiteside won't find you."

At the mention of Representative Dale Whiteside's name, a flicker of hope ignited in my chest. I returned to my cell and wrote to the warden: "Per our conversation sir, I don't know what you're talking about."

Soon after, officers came for me. "Spread eagle, Henderson," they ordered. "We're taking you to the hole."

As they led me away, I made sure others heard me yell, "Call Dale Whiteside! Tell him they're putting me in the hole!"

The lieutenant bellowed, "Shut up! Or you're getting a violation for disobeying a direct order!"

Again, I repeated my yell for someone to call Dale Whiteside—and I was given a violation for disobedience.

As the cell door clanged shut behind me, I closed my eyes and thought of Dale. He was a state representative, and we'd met years ago through another inmate's clemency campaign. From that first meeting, he'd become more than just a useful political contact—he was a true friend and advocate.

I remembered his clockwork visits every other Friday, how we'd talk like old friends. Dale saw me as a woman of substance and strength, despite my circumstances. To him, I mattered as a person, not just a cause.

The next morning, footsteps approached my cell. "Get up, Henderson," the guard said gruffly. "Warden wants you out."

I couldn't help smiling. "Oh, really?"

"Dale Whiteside called," the guard muttered.

As I walked out with my head high, I whispered a silent thank-you. Even the worst abuses in prison could be stopped by small acts of courage from people who cared. In the long, lonely years of prison, true friends were rare gems. And in Dale Whiteside, I'd found the rarest of them all.

But prison had a way of reminding you that safety was always temporary. Just days after Dale's intervention, on what started as another ordinary morning, everything changed. The tennis court—where I walked faithfully every morning—was in sight when a powerful blow struck me from behind. For a moment, the peaceful rhythm of my morning ritual shattered into chaos as I stumbled, my vision blurring. As I turned, I saw her—Marie, a "stud broad" I'd always been friendly with.

Marie stood there, her muscular frame taut with rage. Her short-cropped hair and men's tank top were a stark contrast to my more feminine appearance. In prison, stud broads like Marie often adopted a more masculine style and demeanor, but I'd never felt threatened by her before.

"You b*tch!" she snarled, her fist connecting with my jaw. "You got her transferred!"

I tried to speak, to tell her there had been a misunderstanding, but the punches kept coming. I fell, and her boots found my ribs, my back, my head.

Pain exploded through my skull. As I lay there, my mouth filling with blood, one clear thought repeated: *Jesus, don't let me die. Jesus, don't let me die.*

The yard went eerily quiet. Through swollen eyes, I saw shocked faces watching. I was well-liked; this vicious attack seemed to stun everyone.

Guards rushed in, pulling Marie off me. The guards took me to medical and Marie to the sergeant's office. Then we were separately taken to solitary. Along the way, I heard whispers.

"Why Henderson? She's always fair..."

"It doesn't make sense..."

In the hole, my head throbbed so badly it hurt to lay on the pillow. Days passed in a haze of pain and confusion. When a nurse came to check on me, I asked for a mirror.

She refused. "You don't want to look, Judy," she said softly. "Just trust me. You don't want to look."

As weeks passed, the swelling slowly subsided. I learned the truth: Marie had attacked me over false rumors that I'd arranged her girlfriend's transfer to another housing unit. The misunderstanding had nearly cost me my life.

The attack had the potential to ignite the racial tensions always simmering beneath the surface. I was white, Marie was Black. It was a powder keg waiting to explode.

One afternoon, I approached the warden. "I want to meet with Marie," I said.

He eyed me skeptically. "Are you sure that's wise, Henderson?"

I nodded. "It's necessary."

When Marie entered the room, her eyes widened with surprise. We sat across from each other, the air thick with tension.

"I didn't arrange your girlfriend's transfer," I said quietly. "That was a lie someone told you."

Marie's shoulders slumped. "I...I know that now," she mumbled. "I'm sorry, Judy. I was stupid."

I leaned forward. "We need to fix this, Marie. Not just between us, but for everyone out there. They're ready to go to war over this."

She nodded, understanding dawning in her eyes.

"I'm going to press charges," I continued. "That's my right. But we can still prevent this from getting worse."

I laid out my plan: We would give everyone the impression that we'd buried the hatchet. Marie listened, her brow furrowed. When I finished, she shook her head in disbelief.

"You want us to pretend we're friends? After what I did to you?"

"It's the only way," I insisted. "We walk out of here together, laughing and talking. You help carry my things. We sit in the yard where everyone can see us."

Marie hesitated, then nodded. "Okay. Let's do it."

The next day, we put on our show. As we strolled across the yard, talking, I could feel the stares. Whispers rippled through the crowd.

"Look at Henderson and Marie..."

"I thought they were gonna kill each other..."

We sat on a bench, forcing laughter and animated conversation. Slowly, I felt the tension in the air dissipate.

Later, in my cell, I collapsed on my bunk, exhausted. It had been an act, but it worked. For now, cooler heads had prevailed.

The next morning, I called Dale Whiteside. "I need your help pressing charges," I told him.

"Of course," he replied without hesitation. "I'll be there tomorrow."

As I hung up, I gazed out my cell window. The yard was calm, inmates going about their day. But I knew the peace was fragile. In prison, it always was. Still, I'd done what I could to preserve it, even at great personal cost.

As the dust settled from the incident with Marie, I avoided looking in mirrors. The bruises painted my face in violent shades of purple and yellow—marks I couldn't hide from anyone inside, but I could at least spare my family from seeing.

When the next visiting day approached, I made up excuses. "Tell them I'm not feeling well," I told the guard. "Tell them I'll call instead."

The thought of Angel seeing my battered face, of watching my daughter try to hide her pain—no. I couldn't bear to add to her burden. On the phone, I forced cheerfulness into my voice. "Don't worry about me, baby," I said. "I got this!"

"Are you sure, Mom?" Angel asked, concern threading through her words. "You sound different."

"Just busy with everything here," I replied, the lie tasting bitter on my swollen lips. "How are the kids? How's work?"

As we chatted about family news, I carefully steered the conversation away from my own experiences. The fights, the drugs, the constant tension—I kept it all locked away. Angel's concern was a comfort I couldn't afford. I got this.

Over the years, the thought became second nature: *I'm fine. I got this.* The words felt like a shield, helping me rise above each day's indignities.

One afternoon, a hostile officer shoved me against a wall for no reason. As I picked myself up, I repeated silently, *I got this.*

Weeks later, during a workout, I heard a sickening crack. My foot throbbed with pain, but I gritted my teeth. *I got this.*

Even with a protective boot, I kept leading my aerobics and weight training classes. My students needed me; I wouldn't let them down. *I got this.*

"How do you do it, Miss Judy?" one of them asked after a particularly grueling session. "You never seem to let anything get to you."

I paused, considering my answer. "I just tell myself I got this," I said finally. "And then...I do."

As the words left my mouth, I realized something. Somewhere along the line, the act had become real. The scared woman playing a part had transformed into someone with seemingly endless reserves of strength.

That night, I thought about my family's next visit. I'd put on my usual brave face, tell them everything was fine. But for the first time, I wondered: Was I protecting them, or was I protecting myself?

My mother was battling dementia, and my family moved her to a facility in Scottsdale, Arizona. Her visits became phone calls, but my heart still skipped a beat whenever I heard her voice.

"Judy Cootie-bug!" she'd greet me.

"Hi, Mother," I replied, fighting back tears. Even as Alzheimer's clouded her mind, her love shone through.

Our conversations changed over the years. Sometimes she'd forget where I was, asking when I'd come visit her in Scottsdale. Other times, her clarity surprised me. "Judy Ann," she'd say, her voice suddenly strong, "don't ever give up. You are coming home. God will make sure you come home."

One Sunday, my sister JoElla organized a family conference call. "Let's sing for Mom," she suggested.

And so began our attempt at "Amazing Grace" over four phone lines, scattered across the country. It was like a game of musical telephone gone terribly wrong.

"Amazing grace..." I started, only to hear my brother's voice a beat behind.

"How sweet the sound..." That was Joy, already on the next line.

"...that saved a wretch like me!" my younger sister belted out, completely off-rhythm.

The result was a cacophony of mismatched words and off-key notes. We sounded like a choir of alley cats fighting for the spotlight.

We dissolved into giggles, our failed hymn forgotten. For a moment, I wasn't an inmate. I was just Judy, laughing with her family.

As the call ended, I wiped tears from my eyes—tears of both laughter and longing. Our musical disaster had been just what we all needed.

After the family sing-along, I held on to that warmth, that sense of "I got this" that had carried me through so much. But life has a way of reminding us that sometimes, we don't "got this" at all.

One evening, as I waited for another family call, a guard approached my cell.

"Henderson, phone for you. It's your sister."

My heart raced as I picked up the receiver. JoElla's voice was thick with tears. "Judy...Mother's gone."

The world tilted. I gripped the phone booth, my knees threatening to give way. "No," I whispered. "No, no, no..."

For days after, I was a ghost in my own skin. I sat facing my window, back to the door, refusing food and drink. My mantra of "I got this" felt hollow, meaningless. What was the point of surviving if she wasn't there to cheer me on?

Nights brought no peace, only visions of Mother's kind smile fading to nothing. I curled up like a child, turning to the wall, avoiding everyone.

A week passed before hunger finally drove me from my bunk. Late one night, I crept to the bathroom, hoping to avoid all eyes. As I shuffled back, I passed a cell and heard a voice I knew and disliked.

"Hey, Henderson," she called softly. "You want some chicken?"

I paused, torn. Our history was complicated, our animosity deep. But in that moment, I heard my mother's voice in my head, urging grace. Chicken had been her and my stepdad's favorite meal, after all.

"Sure," I replied, my voice raw from crying.

As we shared the meal, we spoke woman to woman for the first time. Her eyes were kind as she asked, "You wanna talk about her?"

Slowly, haltingly, I began to share. Stories of my mother's laugh, her obsession with cleanliness, her "Judy Cootie-bug" nickname for me.

That night, back in my bed, I whispered into the darkness. "Thank you, God, for the time we had. For letting me care for her with my voice when I couldn't use my hands."

I still missed her fiercely. There was so much left unsaid,

so many adventures we'd never share. But as I drifted off to sleep, I realized something. Maybe "I got this" wasn't about being strong all the time. Maybe it was about accepting help when you needed it, finding grace in unexpected places. And maybe, just maybe, that's what my mother had been trying to teach me all along.

CHAPTER 19

Visions

Twenty-four years into my sentence, I caught a glimpse of Oprah on the common room TV. Her guest was talking about a book called *The Secret*. I leaned in, intrigued despite myself.

That night, one of the book's ideas nagged at me. A vision board, they'd called it. A collage of dreams. I scoffed at first. What good were magazine scraps to a lifer?

But desperation makes fools of us all.

The next day, I started hoarding discarded catalogs. During quiet hours, I'd carefully tear out images, my hands shaking with a strange excitement.

"What are you doing, Henderson?" another inmate asked, eyeing the growing pile of paper on my bunk.

"Just...a project," I mumbled, not ready to share.

Family came first—always did. I placed photos of Angel, Chip, and Mother in the center, their frozen smiles a silent challenge. Around them, I scattered place names like seeds—New York, Africa, Anguilla—hoping they'd take root in reality someday.

Up top, I pasted my wildest dreams: "Free from prison, home with family and friends" and "Sentence overturned, pardoned." The words looked alien there, like they didn't belong. Maybe they didn't.

As I worked, a guard passed by. She paused, peering at my creation. "This is home now, Judy," she said, her eyes sad. "Nobody gets out in Missouri."

I met her gaze. "We'll see," I replied softly.

That night, I tucked the board into my locker, away from prying eyes. Those dreams were too precious, too fragile to share.

In the darkness, I ran my fingers over the photos, willing them to become reality. "I'm coming home," I whispered to Angel's and Chip's smiling faces. "I promise."

Days blended into weeks, into months, into years. On the bad days—and there were many—I'd pull out that board, reminding myself who I was fighting for.

The first few months behind bars, I was all fire and defiance. "I didn't pull the trigger," I'd spit at anyone who'd listen. "I was just Greg's pawn."

But time has a way of clearing your vision.

It was during a session with the prison therapist in Arizona that the first crack appeared in my wall of innocence.

"Tell me about that night, Judy," she said, her voice gentle but probing.

I started my usual spiel, but she interrupted. "No, tell me about you. What were you feeling?"

The question caught me off guard. "I...I was scared," I admitted. "Confused."

"And why do you think you felt that way?"

As we dug deeper, memories surfaced—my father's fists, Charlie's rage, Greg's manipulation. I saw how that pain had twisted me up inside, made me easy prey for Greg.

"Given your history," the therapist asked one day, "was there really any other way that night could've gone?"

The question felt like a punch to the gut. For the first time, I considered that maybe, just maybe, I wasn't entirely blameless.

I had to wrestle with this new perspective—and the truth. Harry was still in the ground, his killer free, and I had a part in that I couldn't run from.

I no longer felt like a victim. But I was still someone who made choices—terrible choices, but choices nonetheless.

"I still think my conviction was wrong," I told the therapist. "The sentence too harsh. But..."

She looked at me, surprised by my hesitation. "But what?"

"But I played a part in this," I finished, the words feeling strange on my tongue.

As the years passed, this realization settled into my bones. We might not pick our circumstances, but we still have to make choices within them. My life had made it hard to stand up to Greg that night, but not impossible.

One day, during a group therapy session, I finally said it out loud. "I had a choice," I admitted, my voice barely above a whisper. "And I chose wrong."

The room fell silent. Then, slowly, other women began to nod. They understood. We all did. True freedom wasn't just about getting out of prison. It was about freeing myself from the chains of denial, one link at a time.

I sat at the worn metal desk, a blank sheet of paper before me. Years into my sentence, I'd joined a program run by the Department of Corrections' Crime Victims Advocacy Group. My task: Write to Harry's family.

My hand trembled as I gripped the pen. I closed my eyes, picturing Harry's face from the few times I'd seen him alive. When I opened them again, my vision blurred with unshed tears.

"Dear Family of Harry," I began, then paused. The advocacy group would scrutinize every word. One misstep, and the letter would never reach its destination.

I poured my heart onto the page, confessing to the pain I'd caused and expressing my deep remorse. As I wrote about understanding the magnitude of their loss, my pen hesitated. How could I truly comprehend their grief? Still, I pressed on, determined to take full responsibility for my role in the tragedy.

Hours passed. I crumpled and discarded draft after draft. Each attempt felt inadequate, hollow against the enormity of what I'd done. Finally, I signed my name at the bottom of the page.

With shaking hands, I sealed the envelope and handed it to the guard. It would go to the crime victims' office for review. Weeks later, I learned they'd approved it for delivery. My words were now in the hands of Harry's siblings—if they chose to read them.

I wondered: Would they open the letter? Would my words bring comfort or reopen old wounds? I knew I had no right to their forgiveness, that my apology might seem trivial compared to their loss.

Yet that letter, inadequate as it was, marked a step toward owning my actions and their far-reaching consequences. It was a reminder that true redemption began with facing the damage I'd done, one painful word at a time.

In 1983, I wrote my first clemency petition. Three pages, each word a desperate plea for freedom. My hand shook as I sealed the envelope.

Weeks later, the rejection arrived. A single sheet of paper, crisp and impersonal. I traced my fingers over the words, "petition denied," feeling my heart sink. But as I crumpled the letter in my fist, something ignited within me. This wasn't the end—it was just the beginning.

I threw myself into studying successful clemency cases, poring over every detail like a scholar deciphering ancient texts. Late into the night, I'd sit cross-legged on my bunk, surrounded by papers, searching for the magic formula that might unlock my cell door.

"Look here," I'd whisper to myself, circling a phrase in a successful petition. "They focused on community service. I can do that."

With each new application, I refined my approach. My life story unfolded on paper, each draft digging deeper into

the painful truths I'd long buried. The abusive relationships, the desperation that led to that fateful night—I laid it
all bare, my pen often pausing as tears blurred my vision.

Hope flickered brightly when I heard about Governor
John Ashcroft freeing two women with life sentences in
Missouri. I pressed my forehead against the cool concrete
wall, closing my eyes and allowing myself to imagine walking free.

But as the years ticked by, that hope began to waver.
Gray streaked my blonde hair, and lines etched themselves
around my eyes—a testament to countless disappoint-
ments.

Then, whispers would ripple through the prison. "Did
you hear? Johnson got out last week. Life sentence, just like
you."

Those stories reignited my determination. I'd return
to my petitions with renewed vigor, meticulously crafting
plans for a future on the outside.

"I could counsel other inmates," I'd mutter, scribbling
furiously. "Use my experience to help addicted mothers
reunite with their kids in foster care."

I learned to show real proof of how I'd changed. Who
was I now, after so long in prison? How would I help society if they let me out? So I detailed every class I'd taken,
every skill I'd honed behind bars. The programs I'd initiated
became points of pride—tangible proof of my growth. When
I spoke to legislators about prison reform, my voice steady
and clear, I made sure to include it in my next petition.

Three times, the parole board recommended my release.
Each time, my heart raced as I awaited the governor's decision. And each time, crushing disappointment followed.

On my darkest days, doubt would creep in like a shadow. I'd stare at my reflection in the mirror, searching for answers in my own tired eyes.

"Have I not changed enough?" I'd whisper, gripping the edge of the sink until my knuckles turned white. "Do I not deserve another chance?"

But even as tears threatened to fall, I'd straighten my shoulders and meet my own gaze with determination. Freedom was out there, and I'd keep reaching for it, petition after petition, year after year. I'd show the world who I truly was, who I'd become—no matter how long it took.

Freedom wasn't just about hope—it was about understanding the system that held me. I signed up for every program the prison offered, but my real goal was mastering the law.

The first time I cracked open a legal text, the words swam before my eyes. "What the hell does 'prima facie' mean?" I muttered, squinting at the page. But I kept at it, day after day, until the jargon became familiar.

I'd fall asleep with case law dancing in my head, wake up reciting statutes. When I aced the paralegal program, I allowed myself a moment of pride. "Not bad for a high school dropout," I grinned, clutching my certificate.

Armed with this new knowledge, I felt ready to take on the world. My lawyer and I would spend hours on the phone, strategizing. My lawyer and I plotted appeals, petitions, and pleas like generals planning a war.

But as appeal after appeal hit dead ends, reality set in.

Knowing the law wasn't a get-out-of-jail-free card. The system was a maze, and I was still stuck in the middle.

Then one day, as I sat in the yard feeling defeated, another inmate approached me. "Hey Judy," she said hesitantly, "I heard you know about this legal stuff. Could you help me with my clemency petition?"

I looked up, seeing the hope in her eyes. "Sure," I heard myself say. "Let's take a look."

Before long, word spread. Women would find me in the cafeteria, slipping me dog-eared paperwork.

"Judy, can you explain this to me?" an inmate would ask, pointing to a confusing paragraph.

"Of course," I'd reply, breaking it down in simple terms.

We'd gather in small groups, huddled over documents. I'd point out key details they'd missed, help them craft compelling narratives.

"Remember," I'd tell them, "no self-pity. Show them how you've changed, what you can offer society."

I'd get on calls with their lawyers, surprised by how often I knew more about clemency than they did.

"You need to emphasize her rehabilitation," I'd explain. "And don't forget to mention the domestic violence—it's crucial context."

The women started standing taller, speaking up for themselves. They'd come to me with grins, waving approved petitions or letters from supportive judges.

"I couldn't have done it without you, Judy," they'd say, eyes shining.

Each small victory felt like my own. My case might've been stuck, but helping these women kept my hope alive. It wasn't just about legal advice. It was about empowerment.

It was about showing these women, hardened by life and beaten down by the system, that they had a right to fight for themselves.

The intercom crackled to life. "Henderson, report to the case worker's office."

My stomach dropped. In prison, unexpected summons rarely brought good news. I shuffled down the corridor, my mind racing through possibilities, each worse than the last.

As I entered the plain room, the lieutenant gestured to the seat across from his desk. His eyes gave nothing away.

"Got something to tell you, Henderson," he finally said. "About that trial years back." He paused before continuing: "One of those girls who was planning to testify on Greg's behalf is back in prison."

"Trina?" I asked in disbelief. That woman's lies had undermined my chance to testify at Greg's trial. She'd said I'd confessed to the murder, and the prosecutor had her and three other women's words against mine.

He nodded. "First thing she did was request protective custody. Said she's afraid of you."

My hands clenched into fists. The nerve, after what she did.

"But here's the interesting part," said the lieutenant, leaning in. "Trina confessed everything to the intake officer. How they were paid to lie about your confession."

The world tilted on its axis. I gripped the arms of the chair to steady myself, my vision blurring.

"She...she admitted it?" I whispered, my voice barely audible.

"Yes ma'am."

A tidal wave of emotions crashed over me. Joy, rage, vindication, disbelief—they warred within me, leaving me breathless. Tears pricked at my eyes, and I blinked them back furiously.

"So what happens now?" I asked, fighting to keep my voice steady.

"We're gonna get Trina to sign an affidavit admitting she lied. Should help your case." He paused. "But only if you keep your cool. No payback."

Part of me wanted to find Trina and shake the truth out of her with my bare hands. But I knew better. I'd waited too long for this moment to mess it up now.

I took a deep breath, forcing my clenched fists to relax. "I understand," I said, meeting the lieutenant's gaze. "One step at a time. The affidavit comes first."

The week after Trina's revelation was a roller coaster. One moment, I'd be scribbling furious letters to the courts, my pen nearly tearing through the paper. The next, I'd collapse onto my bunk, whispering thanks to God that the truth had finally come out.

When the day came for Trina to sign the affidavit, my hands shook as I entered the room. She flinched when she saw me, her eyes darting to the lieutenant standing nearby.

"Hello, Trina," I said, my voice unnaturally calm. "Ready to make things right?"

The scratch of her pen on paper seemed deafening in the silent room. As I signed as a witness, I forced myself to meet her eyes. "Thank you for your honesty," I managed, the words tasting like ash in my mouth.

That night, I stared at the ceiling, my mind racing. After all these years, proof of my innocence existed in black and white.

A few days later, my lawyer, Bob Ramsey, burst into the visiting room, waving the affidavit like a victory flag.

"This changes things, Judy," he beamed, slapping the paper down on the table. "We can petition the court with new evidence now."

For the first time in over two decades, I allowed myself to hope. That piece of paper was our battering ram against the fortress of injustice that had held me for so long.

Five years passed. The wheels of justice turned slowly, but they turned. Then one day, a ghost from the past appeared in the prison yard: Megan, another one of the girls Greg had paid to testify against me.

I almost didn't recognize her at first. She was older, harder, her once-vibrant hair now dull and limp. For a week, I watched her from afar, my emotions churning like a stormy sea.

Finally, I approached her as she sat alone at a picnic table, picking at her food.

"Hey, Megan," I said softly. "It's been a long time."

She wouldn't meet my eyes. "Yeah. Long time, Judy."

I slid onto the bench across from her. "I know what happened with the trial. What they offered you to say I'd confessed."

Megan's shoulders slumped, but she remained silent.

I continued. "I just want to understand why."

Finally, she looked up, her eyes brimming with tears.

"I'm so sorry, Judy," she whispered. "They offered me money and probation. I was weak and scared. I...I didn't think..."

Her words trailed off, but the pain in her eyes spoke volumes. To my surprise, I felt a weight lift from my chest.

"It's okay," I murmured, realizing I meant it. Prison had changed us both.

Megan shook her head violently. "No, it's not okay. I don't deserve your forgiveness. But I'll do anything to make this right."

An idea sparked in my mind. "There is something you can do," I said slowly. "Sign an affidavit telling the truth about their bribes. It could help me get exonerated."

Hope flickered across Megan's face. "Yes, anything. I'll do it right now if I can."

With Trina's confession and now Megan's willingness to come clean, we had real ammunition. The battle wasn't over, but for the first time in decades, I felt like I might just win.

For eighteen years, I watched the seasons change through barred windows, each year marked by a new petition landing on the Missouri governor's desk. With every rejection, I'd go back to the drawing board, refining my words, determined to make someone see the truth.

In the summer of 2000, a spark of hope ignited. Governor Mel Carnahan, a man known for his compassionate approach to clemency cases, took an interest in my story.

One sweltering day, his legal counsel, Joe Bednar,

stepped into the visitation room. My heart raced as I shook his hand—the first time in decades anyone from the governor's office had bothered to meet me face to face.

"Tell me everything, Judy," Bednar said, his eyes kind but probing.

I took a deep breath and began. For hours, I poured out my story. The stenographer's fingers flew across the keys, capturing every word, every tear. As I finished, Bednar leaned forward.

"The governor's considering some pardons in November," he said softly.

My breath caught in my throat. Could this finally be it?

That evening, I called my daughter, Angel. "Mom, this could be it!" she exclaimed. I could hear the smile in her voice. "We're getting your room ready!"

Over the next weeks, I allowed myself to imagine walking out of these gates, hugging my children, sleeping in a real bed.

Then came October 16, 2000. I was folding laundry when the news bulletin flashed across the TV in the common room.

"Governor Mel Carnahan's plane has crashed in Jefferson County..."

I stumbled back to my cell, collapsing onto my bunk. As the full impact hit me, I buried my face in my pillow, muffling my sobs.

The next day, Angel called. Her voice was thick with tears. "Mom, I'm so sorry," she whispered.

"I know, baby," I replied, fighting to keep my voice steady. "It's a terrible tragedy."

We both knew we weren't just mourning Carnahan. We

were mourning the death of a dream, a chance at justice snuffed out on a foggy hillside.

Over the next few days, memories of the past eighteen years flashed through my mind. Each petition, each disappointment, each small victory. They weren't just papers—they were milestones on my journey.

I thought of Governor Carnahan, how he'd taken the time to really see me. In that moment, I realized something meaningful: My voice had been heard. My story had touched someone's heart.

Sitting up, I reached for a pen and paper. It was time to start on the next petition.

CHAPTER 20

Christmas

The day Stacey arrived at Renz Farm in 1992, something stirred in me. She was just a slip of a girl, barely twenty, with haunted eyes that had seen too much. The court had thrown away the key—life without parole for killing her abusive father.

"What're you in for?" she asked me one day in the yard, her voice barely above a whisper.

I gave her the short version. When I finished, she nodded, a glimmer of recognition in her eyes.

"Sounds like we both got dealt a raw hand," she said.

From that day on, we became close. I got to know her family, and I guided her through the clemency process. I started the ball rolling for her, giving her my outline for clemency packets. I saw in Stacey a reflection of my younger self—that same fire, that same hunger for justice. So I took her under my wing, one lifer guiding another.

"You've got to fight, Stacey," I'd tell her during our long talks. "They want us to give up, but we can't let them win."

As the years passed, Stacey's determination grew. We pored over law books together, drafted appeals, and plotted our next moves. Every step forward, I cheered like a proud mama bear. Even when they moved her to another prison, she continued to work on her case.

The day Stacey got her freedom, my heart swelled with pride and a twinge of something else—envy, maybe. But I knew her victory was mine too.

Stacey didn't just survive on the outside—she thrived. When she called to tell me she'd been accepted to law school, I thought I'd misheard.

"Say that again?" I said, pressing the phone harder to my ear.

"I got in, Judy!" she repeated, her voice cracking with joy. "I'm going to be a lawyer!"

I whooped so loud the guard gave me a warning look. "That's my girl," I said, wiping away tears. "You show 'em what you're made of."

Then came the day that changed everything. Stacey called, her words tumbling out in a rush.

"Judy, you're not going to believe this. The governor's office...they've offered me an internship."

For a moment, neither of us spoke. The possibility hung in the air between us, too fragile to acknowledge.

Over the next few months, Stacey became my eyes and ears in the governor's office. She couldn't work directly on my case, but she made sure they knew my name, my story.

"All I can say is that Judy would be worthy," she told them, her voice steady and sure.

Stacey wasn't my only ray of hope. The first time Shannon Norman walked into the prison visiting room, I knew she was different. Her eyes blazed with determination as she extended her hand.

"Judy Henderson? I'm Shannon Norman from Saint Louis University."

I shook her hand, noting her firm grip. "Nice to meet you, Shannon. What brings you here?"

She pulled out a thick folder. "I'm working with Professor John Ammann on the Missouri Battered Women's Clemency Coalition. We're fighting for twelve lifers, including you."

As Shannon spoke, her passion was palpable. This wasn't just another case for her; I could see it in the way she leaned forward, hanging on my every word as I shared my story.

Shannon became a constant in my life. She'd arrive with stacks of papers, her hair disheveled from long nights of research.

One day, as we wrapped up a visit, Shannon hesitated. "Judy, I'm graduating soon," she said, a hint of nervousness in her voice.

My heart sank. I'd grown used to her visits, her determination. "Congratulations," I managed, trying to hide my disappointment.

But Shannon wasn't finished. "I want to take your case with me to my new firm," she blurted out. "I've already asked Professor Ammann. He said yes."

I stared at her, stunned. "You'd do that for me?"

She nodded, her jaw set. "I'm in this for the long haul, Judy. We're going to get you out."

From that moment, I started calling her "the Bulldog." Shannon attacked my case with a ferocity that left me breathless. She navigated the political landscape like a seasoned pro, networking with state senators and representatives at every turn.

One visit, she arrived looking exhausted but triumphant. "I just came from a fundraiser for Senator Johnson," she said, collapsing into the chair across from me. "Made sure to talk to him about your case."

"Shannon, you don't have to—" I started, but she cut me off.

"Yes, I do," she said firmly. "That's how this goes."

But it wasn't just the political game that Shannon mastered. She became a part of my family, forming a bond with my daughter, Angel, that went beyond lawyer and client's family.

As the years passed, Shannon's determination never wavered. Each setback only seemed to fuel her fire. She'd arrive at our visits with new strategies, new angles to pursue.

"We're not giving up, Judy," she'd say, her eyes blazing with that familiar determination. "Not now, not ever."

And despite the years of disappointment, despite the walls that surrounded me, I found myself believing her. With Shannon in my corner, freedom no longer felt like an impossible dream. It felt like a matter of time.

February 21, 2017

That morning, news was breaking across Missouri. A Jewish cemetery in St. Louis had been vandalized overnight. People woke up to find their loved ones' graves turned over, headstones smeared with hate. The whole city was raw with grief and anger.

Missouri's Jewish governor, visibly shaken by the act, responded swiftly. He announced plans to lead a cleanup effort himself, calling on citizens from all corners of the state to join him. It was a rallying cry, a chance to show that Missouri stood united against hatred.

Word of the vandalism and the governor's response spread quickly, even reaching the isolated world of the prison. But it wasn't until my next call with Angel, the same night, that I understood the full impact of that day's events.

"Mom," she began, "you won't believe what happened."

"What is it, honey?"

Angel took a deep breath. "When I heard about the cemetery vandalism, I also found out the governor was organizing a cleanup. Something just clicked, Mom. I knew I had to go."

My eyes widened. "You went to St. Louis?"

"I called off work and just...drove. Four and a half hours straight."

She continued, her words tumbling out faster now: "When I got there, it was chaos. Hundreds of people, news vans everywhere. Even the vice president showed up."

She lowered her voice. "But I didn't care about any of that. I was looking for one person."

"The governor," I whispered, my heart beginning to race.

"It wasn't easy. He was surrounded by Secret Service. This wall of suits and earpieces."

I could see it all so clearly—my daughter, small but fierce, elbowing her way through the crowd.

"I don't know how I did it," Angel said, her voice filled with wonder. "But suddenly, there he was. Right in front of me."

She paused, and I found myself holding my breath. "What happened then?" I prompted gently.

"I reached out, Mom. Right through those Secret Service guys. I grabbed his hand."

I gasped softly, picturing the scene.

"And then I just...I just said it all..." Angel continued. "I said, 'Governor, you have to help my mother. Her name is Judy Henderson. She's in prison for a crime she didn't commit, and her clemency petition is on your desk.'"

For a moment, neither of us spoke.

"Oh, Angel," I whispered, tears pricking my eyes.

"He listened, Mom. He really listened. And he promised his team would look at your file."

I closed my eyes, overwhelmed by the enormity of what my daughter had done.

The months after Angel's encounter with the governor blurred together in a whirlwind of activity. Shannon's visits crackled with excitement and exhaustion.

"Judy, you wouldn't believe it," she'd say. "We're practically living at the governor's office."

I could picture Shannon and Angel, their determination matched only by the dark circles under their eyes, becoming fixtures in the marble halls of power.

"How's it going?" I'd ask, my heart in my throat.

"They're leaving no stone unturned," Shannon would reply. "Justin Smith, the attorney on your case, he's digging deep. And we've got senators casually dropping your name in hallway conversations."

I'd close my eyes, imagining my story echoing through the capitol.

One day, Shannon's voice held a note I hadn't heard before. "Judy, this governor...he's different. He wants his team to read every single page. To really understand your story."

My breath caught. After decades of being a number, someone wanted to see the person behind the file.

"But Shannon." I hesitated. "Isn't it too early in his term? Clemency is usually a last-year thing."

"I know," she said, her voice soft. "That's what makes this so extraordinary."

I tried to temper my hope. I'd been let down by six governors already. But it was hard not to feel a flicker of possibility.

Then came the day I'd been both dreading and longing for. Justin, the governor's attorney, was coming to see me.

As I sat in the visitation room, my hands twisting in my lap, I saw Shannon enter. Her presence steadied me.

"You've got this, Judy," she whispered, squeezing my hand.

Justin walked in, his suit a stark contrast to the drab prison surroundings. He smiled, trying to ease the tension.

"So, Judy," he began, "I hear you've got a spotless record. Well, except for that red light ticket."

I couldn't help but laugh. "It was yellow," I corrected him. "On the way home from the circus with Angel and her friends. Definitely yellow."

His chuckle broke the ice, but his next words sobered me.

"I'm here on behalf of the governor," he said, his tone turning serious. "We want to know who you really are, Judy. I have questions, but I can't make any promises. We're just trying to figure out what to do with your case."

For hours, we delved into my life. Justin asked about everything—the false affidavits, my time in prison, moments I hadn't thought about in years. As Justin began his questions, I watched him scribble notes, adding to the mountain of paper that represented my life. Each answer I gave, each story I shared, was another piece of the puzzle he was trying to solve.

"Tell me about your education in prison," he prompted.

I took a deep breath. "I got my GED, then some college credits. I've been a hairdresser, a paralegal, a dog trainer, even a fitness instructor."

Justin nodded, scribbling more notes. "And the crime itself?"

I met his eyes, steeling myself. "I've never denied my role in what happened. But I didn't pull the trigger, and I've spent every day since trying to make amends."

As our interview wound down, Justin's face was unreadable. "I need to talk with the governor," he said. "No guarantees, but we'll keep you informed."

As the sound of Justin's footsteps faded down the corridor, I was left alone with the weight of possibility. My eyes drifted to the calendar on the wall. December. Another Christmas approached, my thirty-sixth behind bars.

For over three decades, around this time in the calendar, I'd performed the same annual ritual. With mechanical precision, I pulled out the cardboard boxes from under my cot, lining them up like tiny coffins.

"What are you doing, Henderson?" another inmate asked me one year.

I managed a small smile. "Getting ready," I replied, my voice barely above a whisper.

"It's that time again, huh?" she said softly, understanding in her eyes.

I nodded, unable to speak past the lump in my throat.

Christmas was when clemency applicants found out if they were going free. And every year for three decades, I had prepared myself. One by one, I packed away my meager belongings—dog-eared books, creased letters, faded photos. Each item carefully wrapped and tucked away, a life distilled into cardboard containers.

With my space bare, I'd turn toward the small window, imagining the freedom that lay beyond those bars. For a moment, I'd allow myself to picture it: walking out with my boxes, stepping into liberty.

Each year, from Christmas Eve to New Year's, I lived in limbo. My belongings sat packed beneath my bed, ready to leave this place for good. In my mind, I was already gone, starting fresh in a cozy home, reunited with my children.

Each night, I'd whisper my hopes to the darkness. "No more stale prison air come January," I'd murmur. "Just the sweet smell of freedom. This year has to be the one."

But as the days dragged on, no one called my name.

There were no trips to the control center, captain's office, or caseworker—all the places where inmates learn they're getting out. Every year, January 1 came and went.

This year felt different, though. Justin's visit, the thorough review of my case—it all added a new dimension to my annual hope. Yet something held me back. For the first time in thirty-six years, I left my boxes unpacked beneath my bed. Maybe it was exhaustion from decades of disappointment, or maybe some deeper instinct I couldn't name.

As I lay in my bed on a cold night not quite a week before Christmas in 2017, I found myself thinking of Justin poring over those case files, reading every page of my story.

As I drifted off to sleep, I clutched that fragile hope close to my heart. After all these years, all these Christmases, I had never stopped believing that someday, somehow, justice would prevail.

CHAPTER 21

Free

December 20, 2017

"Count time!" the guards barked at 5 a.m., same as every day. I woke up with a jolt. Soon it was time for breakfast. I shuffled to the small table in my cubicle, where a tray of lukewarm oatmeal awaited. As I forced down each tasteless spoonful, I mentally ran through my day's schedule.

That morning, I taught my fitness classes as usual, going through the familiar routines with my students. Then it was off to a clinic visit at eleven o'clock. Then a guard appeared with new instructions.

"Attorney visit," she announced gruffly.

I shook my head. "No, I'm telling you, there has been some mistake. It has to be some other Henderson. My attorney notifies me before—"

"It's for you," the guard cut me off, her tone brooking no argument.

"But—"

"Henderson," she snapped, her patience clearly wearing thin. "You have two choices. Visiting room or lockdown. Pick one."

Swallowing my protests, I nodded and followed her out.

The familiar humiliation of the strip search followed. Cold hands probed and prodded, checking for contraband. As I re-dressed, my mind raced. What was going on? This wasn't a regular visiting day. Had something happened to Angel? To my grandkids?

"Wait here," the guard instructed, gesturing to a hard plastic chair outside the strip room.

Minutes stretched into hours. The tick of the wall clock seemed to echo in the empty corridor. My stomach churned with anxiety.

"Please, God," I whispered, closing my eyes. "Let my family be okay."

The uncertainty was maddening. I'd lived through decades of monotony, but this change in the routine had me on edge. Something was different. Something was happening.

But what?

The guard's voice cut through my spiraling thoughts. "Henderson, your visitor's here."

I stood on shaky legs, my heart pounding against my ribs. As I shuffled toward the visiting room, I tried to prepare myself for whatever awaited me.

The door swung open, and there stood Justin, the governor's attorney. My stomach plummeted. This couldn't be good news. In over three decades of petitions, I'd learned the harsh reality: governors only granted clemency in their final year. This one had barely warmed his seat.

I swallowed hard, steeling myself for the familiar sting of disappointment. Another denial. Another dream shattered. Another return to my cold, gray cell.

"Justin," I managed, my voice barely above a whisper. "What are you doing here?"

He smiled, an oddly mischievous glint in his eye. "Well, there are a couple more questions I want to ask you about your case..."

My heart sank even further. Of course. More questions. More hoops to jump through. More reasons to say no.

"Oh." I sighed, waiting for the axe to fall.

But Justin's smile only grew wider. "Actually," he said, his voice tinged with excitement, "there's someone else here who's been waiting to meet you for a long time."

I stared at him blankly, uncomprehending. Who could possibly be waiting to meet me?

"Turn around," Justin urged gently.

Slowly, as if in a dream, I turned. And there, standing before me, was Missouri's governor, Eric Greitens.

My legs turned to jelly, and I swayed on my feet. The governor reached out, grasping my shoulder to steady me.

"Judy," he said, his voice kind but firm, "it's going to be okay. I'm here to give you good news."

Good news? The words echoed in my head, but I couldn't make sense of them. Thirty-six years of disappointment had conditioned me to expect the worst.

My knees finally gave way, and I sank to the floor. Tears I couldn't control began to flow. Through the blur, I saw the governor kneel beside me, helping me back to my feet.

"I'm here on behalf of the state of Missouri," he said solemnly as we sat down. "I want to apologize for something that should have been corrected many, many years ago."

He pulled out an official-looking document and began to read. My mind struggled to keep up with his words. Then two words cut through the fog: "immediate release."

"Wait," I interrupted, my voice trembling. "Wait. Wait. Wait. Did you say 'immediate release'? As in, right now? Like, today?!"

The governor's chuckle was warm, genuine. "Yes, Judy," he said, his eyes twinkling. "I mean right now."

I sat there, stunned into silence. Right now. After 13,149 days. After 315,576 hours. After 18,934,560 minutes. Freedom was no longer a distant dream, but an immediate reality.

The governor continued speaking, but his words washed over me in a haze. He said something about his team always being there for me, even after my release. I nodded, unable to form coherent thoughts, let alone words.

Then he stood, smiling broadly. "Let me and my team get out of the way," he said. "You have people who have been waiting for this moment a long time."

As if on cue, the door burst open. A flood of familiar faces poured in—my family. My daughter Angel, my sister JoElla, my son Chip, my son-in-law David, my granddaughter Jordan, my grandson Jared, my sister-in-law Tina—all standing in front of me.

We collided in a tangle of arms and tears. Laughter mixed with sobs. Joy intertwined with decades of pent-up grief. The emotions were too big, too complex to name. Shock at the sudden turn of events. Euphoria at the prospect of freedom. Relief that the long nightmare was finally over.

No words were spoken. None were necessary. In that moment, surrounded by the love I'd been denied for so long, I felt a three-decade-old wish become real: I was finally going home.

My final walk through Chillicothe Correctional Center felt like a dream. Each step quivered with anticipation, my world teetering on the brink of transformation. The familiar corridors I'd walked for decades now seemed alien, as if I were seeing them for the first time—and the last.

Memories flooded back with every turn. The cafeteria where I'd shared countless meals with inmates-turned-friends. My cell, where years had slipped away like sand through an hourglass. The room where I'd both received and provided counseling for battered women and incarcerated mothers.

Lining the route to freedom were the people who'd shared my journey—prisoners and guards alike. Some wept openly, others cheered from the tiers. A few offered proud salutes. These were the people I'd fought with, reconciled with, and grown alongside over the years.

I paused to embrace as many as I could, tears flowing freely.

"Thank you," I whispered to some. "Stay strong," I urged others. Our relationships were complex, but genuine. We had suffered together, and I'd earned their respect.

The last face I saw was Pam's—the woman once hired to kill me. Time had melted the ice between us, and by some twist of fate, she was my final embrace before freedom.

Her wide smile sparked something in me. Tears of awe

and gratitude flowed as I recognized how far I'd come. I grasped her hand tightly.

"Pam, I made it!" I cried. "I'm going home."

Pam's eyes shone with joy. "I'm so happy for you, Judy," she replied gently.

As I approached the final door, my family and friends came into view, their faces lighting up with anticipation. My daughter's voice, soft and tender, reached my ears: "Are you ready to take your first steps outside, Mom?"

I nodded eagerly. "I'm ready!" Then, as the enormity of the moment hit me, I hesitated. "Oh my God...I don't know if I am ready!"

I inched forward, each step surreal. My daughter draped my purse over me, a small gesture of normalcy in this extraordinary moment. I clung to my sister JoElla, tears streaming down my face.

To some prison employees nearby, I called out, "It's been fun, girls, but I gotta run! Bye!" Their laughter mingled with my family's, a symphony of joy and disbelief.

As the final door swung open, I gasped. "A limo! Are you serious?!" Outside waited a stretch SUV, rented by my sister—fulfilling a promise made decades ago. "Oh my gosh!" I yelled, the reality of freedom finally sinking in.

I collapsed against my sister, sobbing. "It's happening," I said.

My daughter's voice was soothing in my ear. "It's happened. You're free."

Dale Whiteside held the door as we exited. My attorneys,

Bob and Shannon, stood ready with cameras. "I need a pose!" Shannon cried. I raised an arm triumphantly, grinning skyward. Then I pulled my daughter and sister close, beaming as more family joined the shot.

The winter air hit me like a physical force. For a moment, I couldn't believe I stood under open skies, the prison at my back. Was it real? I inhaled deeply, feeling my spirit expand. The sudden rush of freedom was almost painful, like a deep-sea creature pulled to the surface too quickly.

More Chillicothe staff had gathered to see me off—they'd become family, too, after all these years. Spotting them, I threw my hands up and yelled, "I made it! I'm free!"

The limo's door closed with a soft thud, enveloping me in luxury I'd almost forgotten existed. I ran my hand over the smooth upholstery, marveling at its softness.

As we pulled away, I twisted in my seat for one last look at Chillicothe Correctional Center. A lump formed in my throat—a bittersweet mixture of relief and an emotion I couldn't quite name.

"Goodbye," I whispered, pressing my palm against the window.

The limo hummed to life, and suddenly we were moving. The world outside blurred into colors and shapes I'd almost forgotten existed. Vibrant green trees whizzed by, their leaves dancing in a wind I couldn't feel. Towering buildings reached for the sky, so much taller than I remembered. Billboards flashed by, advertising unfamiliar things—iPhones, Netflix, Twitter.

I fell silent, overwhelmed by the speed, the sights, the sheer vastness of the world I was re-entering. After years of slow-crawling time, this pace was dizzying.

Our first stop was Dale Whiteside's farm in Chillicothe. As we pulled up, I gasped. The yard was filled with people— family, friends, well-wishers. Their cheers erupted as I stepped out of the limo.

"Welcome home, Judy!" they cried, their voices a chorus of joy.

I was engulfed in a sea of hugs, handshakes, and tearful embraces. The air was filled with the scent of home cooking and the sound of laughter. It was almost too much to take in.

"Easy now," Dale said gently, noticing my overwhelmed expression. "Take it slow. You've got all the time in the world now."

Back in the limo, headed to my daughter's home, the motion began to take its toll. My stomach lurched with each turn, unused to the sensation of nighttime travel after so many years of confinement.

"Mom?" My daughter's concerned voice broke through my discomfort. "Are you okay?"

I managed a weak smile. "Just a little carsick, honey. It's been a while since I've been on the road."

She handed me a plastic bag, just in time. "It's okay, Mom. We're almost there."

As we pulled up to my daughter's house, my breath caught in my throat. Cars lined the street, and people filled the yard, cheering my arrival. On the doorstep, I paused.

"What's wrong, Mom?" my daughter asked softly.

I shook my head, tears welling in my eyes. "I . . . I can just open it? No guard, no buzzer? I can just . . . walk through?"

She took my hand, squeezing it gently. "That's right, Mom. You're free now. This is your home."

Inside, the aroma of home-cooked food enveloped me. The dining room table groaned under the weight of dishes I'd almost forgotten existed. But what caught my eye was a bowl of bright red strawberries.

With trembling hands, I picked one up. In prison, fruit was contraband, used to make illicit alcohol. But here, now, it was simply a gift of nature.

I bit into the strawberry, and flavor exploded on my tongue. Sweet, tart, indescribably fresh—it was like tasting color itself.

"Oh," I breathed, tears streaming down my face. "Oh, it's beautiful."

As I savored that single strawberry, I made a silent vow. Never again would I take life's simple pleasures for granted. Each moment, each taste, each freely opened door—these were miracles. And I intended to cherish every single one.

As the last of the well-wishers drifted away, leaving only a handful of family and close friends, my daughter, Angel, gently touched my arm.

"Mom," she said softly, "there's something we want to show you."

She and my sister led me down a hallway, their faces

alight with anticipation. We stopped at a closed door, and Angel squeezed my hand.

"Ready?" she asked.

I nodded, my heart pounding with a mixture of excitement and trepidation. Angel pushed the door open, revealing a cozy bedroom bathed in warm light.

"This is your room, Mom," Angel said, her voice cracking with emotion. "Your very own space."

We stood there for a moment, overcome. Then, as if by unspoken agreement, we all sank onto the bed, sitting cross-legged like we used to do when the kids were small. We talked and laughed, sharing stories and creating new memories to fill the decades-long void.

After what felt like both an eternity and no time at all, Angel yawned. "We should let you rest, Mom," she said, pulling me into a tight hug. "It's been a big day."

With one final embrace, they left, closing the door softly behind them. And suddenly, I was alone.

Despite my bone-deep exhaustion, I couldn't sleep. The bedroom felt strange. It wasn't the lack of comfort that unsettled me, but its abundance.

I ran my hand over the plush comforter, marveling at its softness. The bed seemed to stretch out endlessly, a stark contrast to the narrow one I'd called mine for thirty-six years. I perched on the edge, feeling almost swallowed by its softness.

For a moment, I considered sleeping on the floor. It would be harder, more familiar. Instead, I found myself drawn to the window.

I placed my palm against the cool glass, half-expecting to feel the familiar bite of metal bars. But there was nothing between me and the night sky. I pressed my forehead to the pane, drinking in the sight of stars scattered across the velvet darkness.

"Thirty-six years," I whispered to my reflection. The face that looked back at me was lined with age, hair gray at the temples. I barely recognized myself.

A thirty-two-year-old woman had entered prison decades ago, sentenced to die there. Now, at sixty-eight, I stood on the other side of impossibility. Every breath, every heartbeat, every moment ahead was a gift I'd never expected to receive.

I collapsed into the bed and closed my eyes, overwhelmed by gratitude. "Thank you," I breathed, my words meant for God and for every person who had kept faith when I couldn't. "Thank you for not forgetting me."

Opening my eyes a few hours later, I saw the faintest hint of pink on the horizon. Dawn was approaching, my first sunrise as a free woman in over three decades.

I settled into a chair by the window, determined to greet this new day, this new life, with open arms. The hard years were behind me now. The best, I decided, was yet to come.

CHAPTER 22

Grace

After decades in prison's oppressive grayness, the world erupted into a kaleidoscope of colors and sensations. Things I'd once taken for granted now filled me with child-like wonder.

One afternoon, I found myself in the kitchen, preparing dinner. As the aroma filled the house, I closed my eyes, drinking in the scent of normalcy.

"Mom?" My daughter's voice startled me. "Are you okay?"

I opened my eyes to find her looking at me with concern. "I'm wonderful," I said, smiling through tears. "I'd just forgotten how good cooking smells."

These simple pleasures felt momentous. Long baths seemed to wash away years of sorrow. I lost myself in books, reading late into the night, reveling in the absence of prison's rigid schedule.

"Lights out in five minutes!" I'd sometimes call out to

myself, then laugh at the absurdity of it. Now, I controlled my own time. No more head counts, no more degrading shakedowns. Even brushing my teeth at my own leisurely pace felt like a revolutionary act.

Yet freedom after thirty-six years wasn't the fairy tale some might imagine. I was happy, but I was also disoriented. The world I returned to was strange, transformed beyond recognition.

My children, once little ones I could scoop up in my arms, were now adults with children of their own. Technology that had been the stuff of science fiction was now commonplace. Cultural references flew over my head like birds I couldn't name.

One day, my granddaughter held out a sleek rectangle to me. "Here, Nana, you can use my phone to call Mom."

I stared at it, baffled. "But...where are the buttons?"

She giggled, tapping the screen. It lit up, displaying a keypad. "It's all on the screen, see? You just touch the numbers."

I nodded, trying to mask my confusion. I felt like a time traveler, thrust into an unrecognizable future.

When I began my sentence in the early eighties, computers were rare curiosities glimpsed on TV. The prison offered occasional workshops on these strange machines, which I attended eagerly but left barely wiser.

Later, even these lessons vanished. The system assumed lifers like me would never need such skills. We were expected to die behind bars. Computer classes were reserved for short-timers. The message was clear: Our futures didn't matter.

Now, emerging decades later, I found a world utterly transformed by technology. Clunky PCs had become sleek laptops and smartphones. Words that didn't exist in my vocabulary—apps, Wi-Fi, streaming—now peppered every conversation.

My children patiently explained these technologies, warning of pitfalls. But they'd grown up adapting seamlessly to each innovation. For me, each novelty felt like a confrontation with my own ignorance.

Some days, when my daughter and her husband left for work, I'd sit in their family room and weep. "Maybe I could go back to prison somehow?" I'd wonder aloud, longing for the familiarity of my cell. There, at least, I knew the rules and the lingo.

But with patient guidance, I took each step forward. I mastered rideshares and self-checkout. I learned social media and slang. I tackled computer classes, struggling with this new language.

"You've got this, Nana!" my granddaughter would cheer as I fumbled with a smartphone.

Slowly, I adapted, each small victory a source of pride. I was determined to reinvent myself, not be cowed by change. This wasn't the world I left, but I wasn't the same person either.

The doorbell rang on a crisp morning in 2018. My heart skipped a beat as I opened the door to find a courier holding a manila envelope stamped with the state seal.

"Judy A. Henderson?" he asked.

I nodded, my voice caught in my throat.

"Sign here, please."

With trembling hands, I scrawled my signature and took the envelope. It felt impossibly light for something that carried the weight of thirty-six years.

I called for my daughter. "Angel, it's here."

She rushed to my side as I carefully opened the envelope. The official letterhead swam before my eyes as I unfolded the document within.

"Read it," I whispered, passing it to her. "I can't..."

Angel's voice trembled as she read aloud:

"After examination of the application and the facts relevant thereto, I hereby grant to Judy A. Henderson a full pardon from the above conviction. This pardon obliterates said conviction so that I hereby restore to her all rights of citizenship forfeited by said conviction and remove from her any legal disqualification, impediment, or other legal disadvantage that may be a consequence of said conviction."

The words hung in the air, almost as if I could touch them. More than clemency, this was an acknowledgment of innocence I'd dreamed of for thirty-six Christmases.

"Mom," Angel said, her eyes shining with tears. "It's over. It's really over."

We collapsed into each other's arms, decades of pain and struggle pouring out in a flood of tears and laughter.

As news spread, my phone buzzed incessantly. Friends and supporters called, their joy palpable even through the phone lines.

"This isn't just for me," I told them, my voice thick with emotion. "It's for all of you who stood by me in the darkest times."

That evening, as the house quieted and the initial euphoria settled into a deep, abiding peace, I found myself alone in my room. I knelt beside my bed, the pardon letter clutched to my chest.

"Thank you," I whispered, tears flowing freely. "Thank you for this justice."

As I knelt there, memories washed over me. The countless nights I'd prayed for this moment, the times doubt had threatened to overwhelm me, the small victories that had kept hope alive. The system that had once called me irredeemable now pronounced me redeemed.

Yet as I rose from my knees, a surprising thought struck me. This official vindication, as sweet as it was, wasn't the source of my deepest peace. That had come earlier, in the quiet moments when I'd found contentment within myself, knowing I'd fought the good fight regardless of external validation.

I carefully placed the pardon letter in a drawer and climbed into bed. As I drifted off to sleep, I felt closure. The pardon was a gift, a beautiful affirmation of what I'd always known. But the true freedom, I realized, had come when I'd let go of the need for it.

The first family dinner after my release felt like a scene from a foreign film without subtitles. Familiar faces around the table, yet the dynamics were alien. I fumbled with my fork, watching my grown children navigate the meal with an ease I envied.

"Mom, would you like some more potatoes?" my daughter, Angel, asked.

I nodded, not trusting my voice. As she spooned them onto my plate, I marveled at the woman she'd become. Where was the little girl who used to send me crayon-scrawled cards?

Slowly, we began redrawing our family map. Each interaction was a negotiation of new boundaries and balance. I often found myself turning to my children for guidance, a poignant role reversal.

One afternoon, my daughter was trying to teach me how to use a smartphone.

"Mom, you just swipe like this to unlock it," she explained for the third time.

I fumbled with the screen, feeling like a child. "I'm sorry," I sighed. "I know this must be frustrating for you."

She took my hand, her smile patient. "It's okay, Mom. We've got time. We're learning together."

Those words became our mantra as we navigated this new terrain. Learning together. Whether it was technology, pop culture references, or the intricacies of our evolving relationships, we approached each challenge as a team.

Living with Angel in those early days was a study in contrasts. The child I'd once tucked into bed was now ensuring I had everything I needed.

"Mom, I put fresh towels in your bathroom," she'd say, or, "I picked up some of those vitamins the doctor recommended."

Each act of care was a bittersweet reminder of the years we'd lost.

One rainy afternoon, we found ourselves poring over old photo albums. Angel pointed to a picture of Chip as a toddler, grinning with a missing front tooth.

"He lost that tooth just before a visit with you," she said softly. "He was so excited to show you."

I traced the photo with a trembling finger. "I remember," I whispered. "He was so proud."

We sat in silence for a moment, the weight of lost time hanging between us. Then Angel leaned her head on my shoulder, a gesture so simple yet so profound.

"We can't get those years back," she murmured, "but we're here now. That's what matters."

Our healing wasn't confined to immediate family. At the first extended family gathering after my release, I stood hesitantly at the edge of the room, unsure of my place.

My sister spotted me and crossed the room, pulling me into a tight embrace. "Welcome home," she whispered, her voice thick with emotion.

As the evening progressed, I found myself in conversation with my brother-in-law. "It's been a long time," he said, a hint of awkwardness in his tone.

I nodded, acknowledging the elephant in the room. "I know I can't just slip back into my old role," I said carefully. "But I'm grateful for the chance to try."

These moments of connection, however tentative, were like balm to my soul. They were also reminders of the work still to be done. Trust, I realized, would rebuild slowly, step by step.

Some nights, as I lay in bed reflecting on the day, I'd feel overwhelmed by the enormity of what we were attempting. Rebuilding a family after decades apart was no small feat.

But then I'd remember the laughter at the dinner table, the patience in my daughter's eyes as she taught me something new, the warmth of my family's embrace.

In those moments, I glimpsed the possibility of true forgiveness—not just from my family, but for myself. Our path forward would have its bumps, certainly. But our bond was like a house weathering a storm—the foundation of love remained solid, even as we renovated the rooms of our relationship.

As I drifted off to sleep, I held on to a thought that had become my anchor: Despite our years apart, we'd been given a second chance. My children could have grown bitter, but instead, they welcomed me with open arms. My siblings could have turned away, but they were reaching out, bridging the gap.

This kindness, this willingness to rebuild, was a gift beyond measure. And it was one I vowed never to waste. Together, we would write the next chapter of our family story, one day at a time.

The taste of freedom was still fresh on my tongue when the world ground to a halt in March 2020. As news of the coronavirus pandemic flooded the airwaves, I felt a familiar tightness in my chest.

"Mom," Angel said, her voice tense as she turned up the volume on the TV, "they're announcing lockdowns."

I gripped the arm of the couch, my knuckles turning white. "Lockdowns?" The word hung in the air, heavy with memories I'd tried to leave behind.

Angel turned to me, her eyes filled with concern. "You cannot leave, Mom. It's just for now, until this passes."

Her words, meant to protect, slammed into me like a steel door. In an instant, I was back in my cell, the walls closing in. Angel couldn't know how those well-intentioned words hurled me back into decades of captivity.

As days turned into weeks, and weeks into months, I found myself battling old demons. One morning, I woke in a cold sweat, sheets tangled around my legs.

To combat the creeping anxiety, I fell back on coping tools honed over years behind bars. I'd sit by the window, visualizing the world beyond our four walls.

"There's a park nearby," I'd murmur to myself. "With a pond and ducks. I can go there...when this is over."

When the walls seemed to close in, I'd turn to exercise, pacing the living room like I used to pace my cell. Books became my escape, just as they had been in prison. Meditation, a skill I'd cultivated to survive endless hours of confinement, helped steady me once again.

But some triggers were harder to avoid. One evening, as we watched the nightly news, a government official appeared on-screen.

"As of midnight tonight, all non-essential businesses will be closed..."

I felt my breath catch in my throat, that old feeling of powerlessness washing over me. Angel must have noticed my distress because she quickly changed the channel.

"How about we watch a movie instead?" she suggested gently.

I nodded, grateful for her understanding.

As the lockdown stretched on, the confinement began to wear on me. One day, driven by a desperate need to assert some control, I slipped out to Walmart for medication.

When I returned, Angel was in the kitchen, her face pale with worry. "Mom, did you go to the store today?"

Guilt and defiance warred within me. "I . . . I needed to get out, just for a moment," I admitted.

Angel's shoulders sagged with relief, then tension. "Mom, I understand, but it's not safe. Please, next time tell me. We can figure something out."

Her words, filled with love and concern, helped me realize I wasn't just battling a virus, but the ghosts of past trauma. I had to resist falling into old thought patterns, staying alert to my mind's knee-jerk reactions to confinement.

Over time, with the support of Angel and the rest of my family, I began to reclaim the mental freedom I'd fought so hard for in prison. Each day became a small victory over fear.

The fluorescent lights of Catholic Charities flicker to life as I unlock the front door. It's 7:45 a.m., and I'm the first one here. As I settle behind the reception desk, I can't help but marvel at how far I've come.

"Good morning, Judy!" calls out one of my coworkers as she breezes in. "Ready for another day?"

I smile and nod, grateful for the normalcy of it all. Here, I'm just Judy—not an ex-con, not a former lifer, just a woman doing her job. The fear of being labeled, of being seen only for my past, has faded with each passing day.

Our first visitor of the day enters—an elderly man, his clothes threadbare, his eyes downcast.

"Welcome to Catholic Charities," I say warmly. "How can we help you today?"

As he begins to explain his situation, I feel a familiar tug at my heart. I've been where he is—lost, desperate, in need of a helping hand. As I guide him through the paperwork, I silently say a prayer of thanks for the opportunity to be on this side of the desk now.

The day unfolds in a blur of faces and stories. A young mother seeking food assistance. A veteran struggling with PTSD. An ex-con looking for a second chance. Each one reminds me of why I'm here.

Around mid-morning, a commotion erupts from one of the classrooms. A man's angry voice carries down the hallway. I take a deep breath, steeling myself as I approach.

"Excuse me. Can I help with the situation here?" I ask, stepping into the doorway and assessing the situation. "Sir, would you mind coming with me for a moment?"

The man follows me out, his face twisted with rage. "I don't like the way she talked to me!" he snarls. "I'm a Christian, and I shouldn't have to put up with this! I already did my time! I was captain on my yard in the joint!"

I stand my ground, meeting his gaze steadily. "You know what? You were a captain on your yard. But I was the governor on mine."

His eyes widen in surprise, anger momentarily forgotten.

"So we can deal with this situation in one of two ways," I continue. "Either you can calm down, and we can talk about this as citizens on the street, not prison. Or I can call security and have you escorted out. Which do you prefer?"

As we talk, I see the fight slowly drain out of him. "I'm just trying to get some help," he admits, his voice barely above a whisper.

I nod, understanding all too well. "This isn't the way to do it," I say gently. "You want to change? You want to be different from what you were on that yard? Then you gotta start acting different."

I challenge him to apologize to the class and the instructor. At first, he balks, but something in my eyes convinces him. I watch from the doorway as he swallows his pride and makes amends. He looks both chastened and relieved.

I feel a surge of emotion. This is why I'm here. This is my purpose. This is God's plan.

As I drive home, I reflect on the day. It's not always easy, starting over at my age. There are still moments when I feel out of place, when the weight of my past threatens to overwhelm me. But then I think of the lives I've touched—the elderly man I guided through paperwork, the young mother I comforted, the angry ex-con I helped find a better path.

This isn't just a job. It's a calling. It's my faith in action. As I pull into my driveway, I say a quiet prayer of gratitude. I may not have chosen this path, but I'm exactly where I'm meant to be.

The soft clink of my bracelet against the podium microphone catches my attention. I glance down at the gold band, its engraving catching the light: "She designed the life she loved." My lawyer Shannon gifted me the bracelet and chose the words, and they echo in my mind as I face the sea of expectant faces before me.

"Good afternoon," I begin, my voice steady. "I'm here today to talk about a system many of you have never seen from the inside. But for thirty-six years, it was my entire world."

As I share my story with these lawmakers, I can see the shock in their eyes. It's one thing to read statistics about women in prison; it's another to hear firsthand accounts of missed birthdays, lost decades, and hard-won resilience.

Later that evening, I collapse onto my couch, exhausted but fulfilled. My phone buzzes with a text from Angel: "How'd it go, Mom?"

I smile, typing back: "Great. I think they really listened this time."

My days are full now, in a way I never could have imagined during those long years behind bars. When I'm not working, I'm speaking about my time in prison or helping former inmates navigate the new world they've re-entered.

One Saturday morning, I find myself at a local community center, surrounded by a group of teenagers. Their wary eyes remind me of myself at their age, teetering on the edge of bad decisions.

"Listen," I tell them, leaning in. "I know it feels like the world's against you. But trust me, there's always another way. You have the power to write your own story."

As I speak, I see a flicker of hope in their eyes. It's

moments like these that make every hardship I've endured worthwhile.

But it's not all work. After decades of missed moments, I'm determined to savor every second with my family.

On a warm Sunday afternoon, I sit on a park bench, watching my great-grandchildren play. Their laughter carries on the breeze, a sound sweeter than any I could have imagined during those dark prison nights.

"Nana!" calls out a little voice, my great-grandson running toward me with a dandelion clutched in his chubby fist. "I picked this for you!"

As I pull him into my lap, inhaling the scent of sunshine and innocence, I'm struck by the enormity of this simple moment. This is what freedom truly means.

Later that week, I meet up with an old friend from my prison days who's also been released. We sit in a quaint café, our conversation flowing easily between laughter and reflection.

"Remember when we used to dream about days like this?" she asks, stirring her tea.

I nod, a lump forming in my throat. "Sometimes I still can't believe it's real."

As we chat, I'm struck by how far we've both come. The weight of our past is still there, but it no longer defines us. We're survivors, yes, but we're also so much more.

That night, as I get ready for bed, I catch my reflection in the mirror. The woman staring back at me has eyes that are bright with purpose, with life.

I touch the gold bracelet on my wrist, tracing the engraved words with my finger. "She designed the life she loved." It's not just a pretty phrase anymore. It's a daily choice, a commitment to making every moment count.

There's still so much work to do, so many lives to touch. But there's joy to be found too, in every sunrise, every hug, every small victory.

The past may have stolen years from me, but the future? That's mine to shape. And I intend to make it beautiful.

Choices

Thirty-six years. One-third of a century. An eternity behind bars for a crime I didn't commit.

Outside, life marched on without me. My children, once small enough to fit in my arms, grew into adults. Through sparse visits and treasured letters, I caught glimpses of their lives. My daughter's first day of high school, nervously clutching her backpack. My children's graduations, crossing the stage before an empty chair where I should have sat. First loves, heartbreaks, new jobs—milestones I witnessed only through words on paper and tearful retellings.

As the years passed, my parents aged faster than they should have. Their visits, once regular as clockwork, became rare. The last time I saw my mother, her hands trembled against mine.

Prison stole irreplaceable years. Yet in this place designed to break spirits, I also discovered a deep truth: Even in chains, our choices remain our own.

When strip searches threatened to strip away my dignity,

I chose to see the humanity in the guards, making small talk about weekend plans or favorite books.

In the crushing silence of solitary confinement, I chose to fill the void with whispered stories of hope and redemption.

Faced with the constant threat of violence, I chose peace. I mediated conflicts and taught fellow inmates to read.

These weren't grand gestures. They were quiet, daily choices. Like water wearing away stone, they shaped me. In a place of punishment, I chose growth. In darkness, I learned to create my own light.

To the system, I was just a number. To society, a convicted murderer. But in my heart, I held on to who I really was: a daughter, a mother, a woman of faith.

When freedom finally came—after 13,149 nights—it felt like waking from a long, dark dream. The sun on my face was almost too bright to bear. My family's embrace threatened to overwhelm me with its warmth after so many years of cold.

As I stepped beyond those gates, I held my head high. I wasn't just leaving prison. I was carrying with me a hard-won truth: No matter what life throws at us, we always have the power to choose who we become in the darkness. And when we make that choice, we can welcome the light when it finds us again at last.

Acknowledgments

This book is a tribute to the many people who stood by me during my darkest hours. Their kindness and courage shine like threads of gold in the fabric of my story.

To my children: Angel, your love and tireless fight for my freedom guided me through the years. Your strength in pursuing your dreams, despite my absence, fills me with pride. Chip, I'll never forget your bravery at sixteen, driving yourself to the prison to see me after eleven years apart.

To my family: My siblings, my late mother, and my stepfather, you were my rock. Mother, you never let me give up hope. Dad, thank you for the kindness you showed in your later years, helping to mend our relationship.

To my friends: Your loyalty through long silences between letters and calls kept me going. I'm especially grateful to those who investigated my case, organized rallies, and fought for my release. Dale Whiteside, I owe you a debt I can never repay.

To my prison family: The bonds we formed are unbreakable. You're forever in my heart.

To the compassionate staff: Thank you—especially you, Sergeant Ponder—for seeing my humanity amidst the harshness of prison life. And to my caseworker, Marty Wood, who always kept me encouraged and said she'd never retire until I was free. (She finally did retire—in July 2018, seven months after my release.)

To my legal team: Robert Ramsey, John Ammann, Shannon "Bulldog" Norman, and others—your persistence against the odds amazes me. Tom Mountjoy, your courage to speak up—as a prosecutor—made a difference.

To those who secured my freedom: Governor Eric Greitens and his team, particularly Justin Smith and Lucinda Luetkemeyer—your bold action gave me back my life and my family. I will be forever thankful.

To those who brought this book to life: Jimmy Soni, your unwavering advocacy over six years made this story possible. Whitney Gossett, your belief in this project opened doors. Jenny Baumgartner and her editorial team, your expertise shaped these pages.

To my grandchildren and great-grandchildren: May my journey light your path forward. Know that my love surrounds you always, and remember—nothing is impossible.

Each person mentioned here, and many more, played a crucial role in my journey to freedom. My gratitude is beyond words. This book is my attempt to repay that debt and to show the power of perseverance, compassion, and the human spirit.

This story belongs to all of you who champion the forgotten, who see the person behind the prisoner, who fight tirelessly for what's right. Thank you for keeping hope alive when all seemed lost.

May your kindness continue to light the way for others, as it has done for me.

About the Authors

Judy Henderson is a prominent advocate for criminal justice reform and women's rights. She was wrongfully convicted of murder in 1983 and spent over thirty years in the Missouri prison system before her release in 2017.

While incarcerated, Judy became a dedicated activist and outspoken critic of abuses within the prison system. She led campaigns for legislation to recognize battered woman syndrome as a legal defense, and she spearheaded programs to help mothers in prison maintain connections with their children. Her courageous work earned Judy broad respect among policymakers, attorneys, and fellow inmates.

Since her release, Judy has continued her justice reform advocacy beyond prison walls. She frequently speaks on panels, gives media interviews, and meets with legislators to provide insights only possible from her firsthand experience. Judy also volunteers with groups that support former inmates' successful reentry to society.

Judy resides in Missouri near her loving family and works at Catholic Charities. Though she lost decades of precious time, Judy maintains a powerful spirit and continues working to transform hardship into positive change. She demonstrates every day that no matter how broken the system, one courageous voice can still ignite reform. To learn more about Judy and to connect with her, please visit www.judyannhenderson.com.

Jimmy Soni is an award-winning author and a sought-after ghostwriter and speechwriter. His latest book, *The Founders: The Story of PayPal and the Entrepreneurs Who Shaped Silicon Valley*, was a national best-seller and named one of the best books of the year by *The New Yorker*, among other accolades.

As a ghostwriter and speechwriter, his words have been read and heard by millions, and several of his ghostwritten books have become #1 *New York Times* best-sellers. He has written for the nation's leading public officials, CEOs, prominent athletes, media moguls, Hollywood personalities, and nonprofit leaders.

He lives in Brooklyn, New York, with his daughter, Venice. You can learn more about his work at jimmysoni.com or follow him on Twitter/X.com at @jimmyasoni.